YOU'RE
NOT AS
CRAZY
AS I
THINK

YOU'RE NOT AS **CRAZY** AS I THINK

Dialogue in a World of Loud Voices and Hardened Opinions

RANDAL RAUSER

Biblica™ Transforming lives through God's Word

Transforming lives through God's Word

Biblica provides God's Word to people through translation, publishing and Bible engagement in Africa, Asia Pacific, Europe, Latin American, Middle East, and North America. Through its worldwide reach, Biblica engages people with God's Word so that their lives are transformed through a relationship with Jesus Christ.

Biblica Publishing
We welcome your questions and comments.

1820 Jet Stream Drive, Colorado Springs, CO 80921 USA
www.Biblica.com

You're Not as Crazy as I Think
ISBN-13: 978-1-60657-093-7

13 12 11 / 6 5 4 3 2 1

Printed in the United States of America

CONTENTS

ACKNOWLEDGMENTS

Width some trepidation I traveled to Calgary, Alberta, in February 2009 to deliver an address to the Association of Christian Schools International (ACSI) Alberta Educator Convention, which was evocatively titled "Brainwashed? On the Challenge of Christian Education." Though I may have heralded some reservations going in, the challenging and engaging discussion that followed convinced me of the need to write the present book. And so I extend my thanks to all those who were present at that talk and shared their well-considered opinions and questions. Next, thanks to Biblica Publishing and in particular to publisher Volney James, who readily issued a contract and provided encouragement throughout the writing and editorial process, and to the editorial work of Bette Smyth. Thanks also go to my wife, Rae Kyung (Jasper), and daughter Jamie, who showed eminent patience throughout the writing process (to the point where I even dared to bring my netbook to the dinner table!). Finally, thanks to Anne Rauser (my mom) and to Rick Rauser (my brother), who both read the entire manuscript and offered many helpful comments.

For Rick

Brother, Friend,

and Truth Seeker

1

WHO NEEDS TRUTH WHEN **YOU'VE GOT** JESUS?

Woody Allen's film *Crimes and Misdemeanors* tells the disturbing story of ophthalmologist Judah Rosenthal (Martin Landau). Although Rosenthal has a serene life, it begins to unravel when he has an affair with a flight attendant. Rosenthal thinks he can lead a comfortable double life—until his mistress resolves to tell his wife of the affair in a move that will ensure the destruction of his family. When all attempts to keep her from talking fail, Rosenthal resorts to hiring a contract killer in order to have her murdered. After the dark deed has been completed, he surreptitiously returns to her apartment. As he gazes on her lifeless body, the gravity of his crime begins to sink in. Some weeks later the growing guilt Rosenthal struggles with drives him back to the home of his youth in search of some kind of solace and guidance. As he wanders through the house, he pauses at the dining room while memories of a busy Passover Seder from his childhood begin to flood back. As the scene unfolds in his memory, Rosenthal's father, Sol, is dutifully leading the service when his secular aunt May rudely interrupts the "mumbo jumbo" proceedings. May's condescending dismissal of Sol's piety prompts a debate among the guests concerning the rationality of belief in God in the modern world. When one of the men at the table asks Sol what he would say if it turned out that his faith was wrong, Sol resolutely replies that even if he is wrong, he will still have lived a better life than the unbeliever. This prompts an indignant retort from May: "Wait a minute. Are you telling me that you prefer God to the truth?" Sol's answer is instant and resolute: "If necessary I will always choose God over truth!"[1]

I believe that this little story provides a sobering parable for the state of much of contemporary evangelicalism. The dining room table represents the public square of debate and discourse, a table that bustles with the views of secularists, atheists, humanists, Muslims, pluralists, Buddhists, and many others. Evangelicals have long seen their role at the table in much the same way that Sol views his, as defenders of the one truth against a world of error and skepticism. In the midst of the cacophony of civil and uncivil exchange, the evangelical soldiers on. Even as he faces critique and occasionally even mockery, still he strives valiantly to defend the gospel. The commitment of evangelicals to this fight has occasionally waned as they have been drawn by the lure of more worldly pursuits.[2] However, in the last decade a number of evangelical voices have expressed a renewed dedication to the importance of truth for the wider community. For evidence of this trend, consider the spate of recent books evangelicals have published on truth in the last decade, including *The Truth War; Culture Shift: Engaging Current Issues with Timeless Truth; Total Truth; Evangelical Truth; Time for Truth; Truth Decay; Whatever Happened to Truth; The Wedge of Truth; Truth and the New Kind of Christian*; and (my favorite title) *True Truth*.[3] And to cap it off, in 2006 Focus on the

---

1. For an astute discussion see Sander H. Lee, "If Necessary I Will Always Choose God over Truth!" *Woody Allen's Angst: Philosophical Commentaries on His Serious Films* (Jefferson, NC: McFarland, 1997), 255–89.

2. For a discussion see David Wells, *No Place for Truth, or, Whatever Happened to Evangelical Theology?* (Grand Rapids, MI: Eerdmans, 1993).

3. See John MacArthur, *The Truth War: Fighting for Certainty in an Age of Deception* (Nashville: Thomas Nelson, 2007); Albert Mohler, *Culture Shift: Engaging Current*

Family released a complete worldview curriculum entitled *Focus on the Family's The Truth Project*®, a watershed of unprecedented scope and ambition intended to ignite the church's passion for truth. All told, the evidence suggests that evangelicals are showing clear signs of Sol's dedication to standing for the truth.

But what about the negative side of Sol's witness? Is there evidence that evangelicals have abandoned the virtuous pursuit of truth for the sake of defending their own beliefs, true or not? Certainly this appears to be the widespread assumption among non-evangelicals, as Joel Kilpatrick suggested in his satirical book *A Field Guide to Evangelicals and Their Habitat*: "The purpose of evangelical education, like the purpose of Fox News, is to dispense with contradictory ideas with as little thought as possible, resulting in eighteen-year-old biblically literate virgins who vote Republican."[4] Whether or not this is a fair characterization of evangelical education, Kilpatrick's satirical description accurately reflects a common *perception* about it. Despite all this talk of truth among evangelicals, many others at the table suspect that they are really more concerned with perpetuating their own sectarian ideology.[5] So despite the fact that evangelicals loudly proclaim their

---

Issues with Timeless Truth (Colorado Springs, CO: Multnomah Books, 2008); Nancy R. Pearcey, *Total Truth: Liberating Christianity from Its Cultural Captivity* (Wheaton, IL: Crossway Books, 2004); *Evangelical Truth: A Personal Plea for Unity, Integrity & Faithfulness* (Downers Grove, IL: InterVarsity Press, 1999); Os Guinness, *Time for Truth: Living Free in a World of Lies, Hype, and Spin* (Grand Rapids, MI: Baker, 2002); John Stott, Douglas R. Groothuis, *Truth Decay: Defending Christianity against the Challenges of Postmodernism* (Downers Grove, IL: InterVarsity Press, 2000); R. Albert Mohler et al, *Whatever Happened to Truth* (Wheaton, IL: Crossway, 2005); Philip E. Johnson, *The Wedge of Truth: Splitting the Foundations of Naturalism* (Downers Grove, Il: InterVarsity Press, 2002); R. Scott Smith, *Truth and the New Kind of Christian* (Wheaton, IL: Crossway, 2005); Art Lindsley, *True Truth: Defending Absolute Truth in a Relativistic World* (Downers Grove, IL: InterVarsity Press, 2004).

4. *A Field Guide to Evangelicals and Their Habitat* (New York: Harper SanFrancisco, 2006), 131.

5. In his incendiary book *American Fascists: The Christian Right and the War on America*, Chris Hedges warned that homeschooled evangelical children "are taught, in short, to obey. They are discouraged from critical analysis, questioning and independent thought.

fidelity to truth, critics suspect that they reflect nothing more than Sol's misguided piety: "If necessary I will always choose God over truth!"

Even if people have the impression that evangelicals are willing to sacrifice truth for the sake of their beliefs, surely the deeper question is to ask whether this is in fact true. In this book I will argue that it is indeed often true, certainly more so than evangelicals are typically willing to admit. Time and again we have revealed ourselves to be more interested in defending and perpetuating our beliefs on a given issue than in discerning where the truth really lies. Often we have preferred to secure our present beliefs against challenge rather than to embrace the open risk of real dialogue. Even if we would never come out and say that we choose anything, even God, over truth (after all, what would that even *mean*?), our actions often suggest otherwise. As a result, actions that may have been intended to secure the faith from attack instead undermine our witness to others gathered at the table, leaving them to conclude that we are not that serious about truth after all but are simply pushing an "agenda." And this ultimately leaves the evangelical's stance looking as ironic and pathetic as the beleaguered rabbi in Allen's film.

This brings me to the second part of my thesis. If we have often shown ourselves to be less than diligent pursuers of truth, the solution is straightforward, if not simple: we need to be doers of the truth and not hearers only. And this means developing the character and traits that always seek after truth in all things. With that in mind, my goal in this book can be stated as follows: *to challenge evangelicals, other Christians, and everybody else to develop characters of truth that are in harmony with their proclamations of truth.* At a pluralist table crowded with various opinions, where reasoned civil discourse is often

---

And they believe, by the time they are done, a host of myths designed to destroy the open, pluralist society" (New York: Free Press, 2006), 26.

trumped in favor of quick sound bites, we need now more than ever to be faithful disciples of truth.

Since it is important to keep this kind of discussion grounded in concrete reality, I will link my frequent engagement with evangelical attitudes toward truth with respect to a very real, even if fictional, evangelical who embodies both the nobler characteristics and attendant weaknesses of the tradition. His name is Ted, and he is a forty-something evangelical who lives somewhere in the Bible Belt, USA. Ted converted to Christ while attending a university twenty years ago; he is married, has two children in college, and owns his own sporting goods shop. Ted regularly takes the family out to Dairy Queen after Tuesday night Bible study, ushers twice a month, and is a genuinely nice guy. He also reads widely, especially in areas like apologetics and evangelism. While he loves his work, he views his primary calling as that of an evangelist, though his style is typified more by soft conversations that lead into matters of eternal significance than by in-your-face questions like "Do you know where you'd go if you died tonight?" Ted may love sports, his country, and his family, but he'll tell you that he loves the truth most of all. All this is important because, far from being a caricature of our weakest link, Ted is a thoughtful, educated, and amiable Christian. Indeed, he is just the kind of individual most pastors would love to recruit as a deacon or adult Sunday school teacher (Ted is both). So, to the extent that Ted comes up short in the rigorous pursuit of truth, it is a reflection on, and indictment of, the wider evangelical community. With this in mind we will often return to consider Ted's opinions at various points in the book. But before we get started, I will take a few moments to provide a brief overview of the road ahead.

Getting Serious about Truth

Our inquiry into truth shall unfold in two parts. In chapters two through six we will seek to identify core assumptions and practices that tend to inhibit our pursuit of the truth, as well as those that aid us in realizing the pursuit of truth. This will provide the foundation for the series of four dialogues that we will undertake in chapters seven through ten.

The discussion shall commence in chapter two, "Truth Is Who You Are," where we will begin by considering the concept of truth as a quality that applies not only to statements but also to persons. Sadly, evangelicals have often had the wrong idea about what a character formed by truth looks like. For instance, they have often located the truthful character in the voice that speaks with the greatest passion, conviction, and simplicity or clarity of vision. But if we have passion, conviction, and simplicity without the subtler virtues to be examined in chapters three through six, our advocacy for truth could be subverted even with the best of intentions. And this would leave us perilously close to Sol's dogged defense of his beliefs.

It can be unsettling to admit that our grasp of truth is always a work in progress. Especially disconcerting is the notion that part of the commitment to pursuing truth is the willingness to rethink even our core fundamental beliefs. Interestingly, the Christian might worry that this willingness to pursue truth wherever it leads could constitute a form of betrayal. After all, aren't we to treat Christ as supreme over all other things? So how could we countenance the possibility of rethinking—or even rejecting—the very individual who demands our supreme commitment? If we believe that Jesus is the truth, then how could we consider the possibility of rejecting Jesus as an act of fidelity to the truth? While I readily understand Ted's reservations at this point, my response shall come in chapter three: "If Jesus Were Not the Truth, He'd Be the First Person to Tell You to Look Elsewhere."

We all have a built-in tendency to retain and protect our beliefs even when the evidence begins to mount against them. One way to protect our beliefs in the teeth of such challenges is by reducing the often bewildering patina of reality to a stark range of either/or positions like good or evil, right or wrong, and true or false, while stressing that *our* beliefs are the good, right and true. Like most Christians, Ted is also prone to lapse into these simplistic binary opposites. So Ted often protects his beliefs by assuming that his own position is the completely good, right, and/or true one, while the opposing view is completely evil, wrong, and/or false. Unfortunately, reality is rarely this simple, and to insist that it is will inevitably lead to a range of distortions. In chapter four, "Not Everything Is Black and White," I will argue that these kinds of binary oppositions are indefensibly oversimplified and inhibit critical thinking. The person who has a character formed by truth will forgo such oversimplified distortions and instead embrace the inevitable complexity and ambiguity of truth.

When Ted views issues in black-and-white terms and assumes that the evidence unequivocally supports his position, he is left with a practical problem: How can he explain the fact that decent, rational people continue to disagree with him? When boiled down to essentials, the answer seems to be that such disagreement must arise from some serious intellectual or moral deficit on the part of the detractor: that is, if truth really is this simple, then the person who continues to disagree with Ted (or you or me, for that matter) is either ignorant of the relevant evidence or aware of it but maliciously refusing to acknowledge it. While this *may* be true in some exceptional cases (there are a few crazy and wicked people out there), it surely is an implausible way to explain most cases of ongoing disagreement. Or so I shall argue in chapter five, "Those I Disagree with Are Probably Not Ignorant, Idiotic, Insane, or Immoral."

While Ted loves to engage others in discussions of truth, rarely does he enter a conversation with a real openness to being converted by the other. When he asks people to share their opinions, he listens politely, but he doesn't listen *well*. Truth be known, he really cannot wait for them to finish so that he can share his perspective, the *right* perspective. Let's not judge Ted too harshly here, for it surely is hard to listen to others share their beliefs when you are convinced that they are plain wrong and that you are perfectly right. But what happens when we admit that disagreement arises not only because of an intellectual or moral deficit on the part of our detractors? What if we admit that sometimes they may have *good* reasons to disagree with us? Let's go further: Could it be (dare we think it?) that the reasons they have for their position might sometimes be at least as legitimate as the reasons we have for ours? Perhaps even more so? In chapter six, "This Conversation Could Change Your Life," we will consider how a truthful character commits us to the hospitality and vulnerability of openly listening to others.

Truth in Conversation

By now it should be clear that commitment to the truth means much more than a dogged adherence to the set of statements we happen to believe. A commitment to truth is also a character-forming commitment to know reality as it is revealed in the world and our interaction with others. So, a close-minded refusal to hear the truth in others is incompatible with being people of truth. The real person of truth is one who expresses a genuine willingness to listen to the other as an equal conversation partner. That is precisely what we will begin to do in the second section as we engage in a series of conversations with four groups that are often marginalized by evangelicals: liberal Christians, Darwinists, animal rights activists, and atheists.

We will begin with Ted's hostility toward so-called liberal Christians. For Ted, much of that hostility is directed at St. Joseph's, the small Episcopalian church that he passes every day on his way to work. Ted takes a certain pride in the striking contrast between that tiny communion and the gigantic and ostentatious suburban evangelical church that he attends, with its sprawling campus, sparkling café, and spectacular fountains. While St. Joe's is the frequent butt of Ted's jokes, beneath the humor lies deep puzzlement at, and even hostility toward, the Christian liberalism that it represents. Ted has heard that St Joe's counts the local abortion doctor and a number of practicing gays among its congregants. And Ted has doubts about its priest (or priestess?), a woman with short hair he saw at last year's missions conference. After hearing her open the morning session by *reading* a prayer out of a book, Ted whispered to his friend: "Is it any surprise that St. Joe's is dead? They can't even *pray* in their own words." But is that a fair assessment of St. Joe's specifically and liberal Christianity more generally? We shall explore this question in chapter seven, "Not All Liberal Christians Are Heretics."

While Ted harbors some antipathy toward St. Joseph's, the controversies raised by liberal Christianity have never entered his comfortable home. But another issue blew up this past Thanksgiving at the dinner table. Mark, Ted's son, had returned from his first semester of college just hours before. Suddenly, right there over turkey and gravy, the boy started spouting off nonsense about how the scientific evidence shows that we are descended from monkeys. And to make matters worse, the kid then had the nerve to suggest that this ridiculous theory of evolution didn't contradict the Bible. "I'm not descended from a monkey!" Ted snapped back. "And I'm not going to let an evolutionist make me into one." So shaken was Ted at Mark's flirtation with Charles Darwin that he even declined his usual second helping of pumpkin pie. While this conflict may have led to a rather icy Thanksgiving, Ted and Mark are not alone. Indeed, this same debate over origins has wreaked havoc at many Thanksgiving tables as Christian students have returned from universities with newly discovered ideas that challenge the deeply held convictions of their parents. We will enter into the thick of this debate in chapter eight as we consider the claim that "Not All Darwinists Are Monkeys."

Even if Mark is entertaining some pretty wild ideas, Ted is confident that the boy will sort himself out soon enough. (The creationist book that Ted slipped into Mark's suitcase before he headed back to school should help.) In the meantime, Ted has a wonderful and supportive neighborhood. Just across the street there is a great Baptist family and a fine young Pentecostal couple. And even if the neighbors on the north side are Mormons, they're decent enough folk. Indeed, they even lent Ted's family their motor home for a trip to the Grand Canyon last summer. Unfortunately, things are not quite as congenial with the neighbors on the south side. Both of them are animal rights wackos, who, according to Ted, "care more about an unborn eaglet than an unborn baby." Their sense of moral superiority is so overbearing that Ted's wife has even become uncomfortable wearing the fur he bought her for their fifteenth anniversary (a fact that Ted deeply resents). And you cannot imagine their sanctimonious glances over the fence every time Ted invites his small group from church over for a backyard barbeque. Still, he must admit to getting a certain wicked satisfaction in cutting into a juicy steak, knowing that those tofu-eating nut jobs are silently glaring from their patio. With so much enmity, is it possible to save Ted's relationship with his animal-loving neighbors? Even if Ted cannot convince them to try a piece of his triple-A prime rib, might they persuade him to sample a cube of their tofu? We'll turn to address this topic in chapter nine, "Not All Animal Rights Activists Are Wackos."

Liberal Christians, Darwinists, and animal rights activists—this is a pretty ignominious list for your average conservative, Bible-believing Christian. But every one of them would probably have a better image than our last interlocutor: the atheist. And this is hardly surprising. After all, while these other groups take a stand on a relatively peripheral issue, the atheist denies the most basic Christian confession of all: the existence of God. If you want Ted's opinion on atheism, ask him about the fellow he interviewed last fall for a sales position at his sporting goods store. The interview with this fellow—Osman was his name—started out with promise, given his impeccable resumé and clean-cut image. But things quickly began to go downhill when Ted inquired about one entry on Osman's resumé under "community service": his role as volunteer secretary for a local freethinker society. As soon as Osman explained that he was an atheist, Ted immediately determined to throw his application into the trash. What else could he do? After all, the Bible declares the atheist a fool (Psalm 14:1), and one of the few things more foolish than being a fool is hiring one. Case closed? Or is it just possible that not all atheists are fools? That question shall occupy us in chapter ten.

Coda

In each of these four conversations we are seeking to develop the disciplines of charity that go with a character formed by truth. In each case the modus operandi involves a resolution to engage with the other—the liberal, the Darwinist, the animal rights activist, and the atheist—as an equal partner in dialogue and so to treat each one as a person we can learn from and need to listen to. Given the overriding human penchant for responding defensively to those we disagree with, this discipline of listening is an uncommon, even revolutionary, notion.

If you'd like a metaphor for the unfolding conversation, I would suggest that we switch from the roundtable of debate to the battlefield. But not just any battlefield. I am thinking in particular of the 2005 film *Joyeux Noël*, which tells the incredible story of the spontaneous Christmas 1914 truce in World War I that arose on the battlefield between German, Scottish, and French troops. The cease-fire began in an impromptu way on Christmas Eve when some of the Scots pulled out their bagpipes and began to lead their fellow soldiers in some festive carol singing. Then from the opposite end of the battlefield the voice of a German opera star responded with a haunting rendition of "Adeste Fideles" that rang out over the wasteland of frozen mud and barbed wire. These modest gestures of common humanity in a time of unremitting hostility culminated on Christmas Day with the officers of both sides laying down weapons and meeting together to formalize a temporary cease-fire and share a holiday of peace on earth, goodwill toward men.

As promising as the story is, the end of *Joyeux Noël* is bittersweet, for once the holiday is over the cease-fire goes with it as the soldiers return to their respective ditches and resume the senseless battle. At that point we must part ways with the illustration, for I am not calling for a temporary cease-fire on the battlefield of ideas followed by a return to the comfortable confines of the close-minded defense of party lines, of all against one and one against all. Rather, I am calling for an enduring truce based on a mutually shared desire to know the truth. It is a truce that we adopt not because we are weak or cowardly or lacking in the courage of our convictions. Rather, it is a truce rooted in the fact that our deepest conviction ought to be the desire to know the truth, as well as the willingness to see this same conviction in our "enemies." For too long we have objectified the dissenting voice at the other end of the battlefield as nothing more than a target of conquest. But what if we lowered our rhetorical guns and climbed out of the ditch of our entrenched opinions to join the "enemy" on the field of common humanity, united in our love for and pursuit of the truth? This book offers the first modest steps toward just such a grand vision.

2

TRUTH IS
WHO
YOU ARE

A few years ago, back when Dan Brown's *The Da Vinci Code* was at the height of its popularity, I delivered a number of public lectures critiquing the book's tendentious historical claims. Near the beginning of one of those lectures, just as I was starting to explain how historians reconstruct the past, a hand went up in the audience. Given that I had hardly said anything at this point, I was a bit surprised to see a question so early. But I was even more surprised when the young man then blurted his question out abruptly: "*What is truth?*" Judging by some of the confused glances from others in the audience, I suspected that many people did not appreciate the relevance and/or depth of the question. After all, they had come to hear about *The Da Vinci Code,* not some highfalutin, philosophical expostulations on the nature of truth. But even if we might have questioned whether this was the most appropriate moment for the young man's query, I had little doubt that this would be the most profound and far-reaching question to be asked that morning. And this is hardly surprising, for it is a question with an impeccable historical pedigree, since it is the very same query that Pilate memorably posed to Jesus two millennia ago (John 18:38), and it has attracted the interest of thoughtful people ever since.

The nature of truth is so important that we will devote this chapter to the concept. In particular, we shall focus on how truth is both a relationship that correct statements bear to reality and a relationship that we bear to Jesus Christ. This means that we need to seek not only to acquire beliefs that are true but also to be truthful people. Unfortunately, when we look for others who might be trustworthy guides for truth, we are often drawn more to style than substance. This becomes evident when we identity a truthful character simply with passion, conviction, and a simplicity of vision. These characteristics can be valuable so long as they come with the characteristics to be examined in chapters three through six. However, apart from those virtues they can lead people to emulate a combative warlike ethos that quickly becomes the enemy of truth.

Seeking the Truth about Truth

My guess is that the man who asks, "What is time?" at a cuckoo clock convention would not be particularly well received by those gathered to hear about the latest advances in pipes and pendulums. So it is for the man who dares to ask, "What is truth?" at a *Da Vinci Code* lecture. And yet, this seemingly abstract and impractical question is important, and we overlook it at our peril. Indeed, a person's view of truth is like the rudder on a large ship: it may lie beneath the surface most of the time, but it determines the direction of the massive vessel. For that reason, in this chapter we will pull the liner into dry dock for a closer inspection.

Let's begin with the basics. When we inquire into the nature of truth, we find ourselves in the company of many of history's great philosophical minds. The ancient Greek philosopher Aristotle provided an enormously influential definition of truth more than 2,400 years ago when he wrote the following: "To say of what is, that it is, and of what is not, that it is not, is true."[1] While Aristotle probably didn't win any poetry contests with this definition, at least it has the virtue of being to the point and containing more good sense than the more extreme postmodernists: truth consists in speaking accurately of the way things are. This has been called the correspondence theory of truth because it roots truth in the correspondence between a statement and the state of affairs that the statement describes. More tersely, truth is the property of statements that accurately describe reality. For instance, the statement "it is sunny out" is true if and only if it is sunny out. And the statement that "there are more existentialist philosophers in Paris, France, than in Paris, Texas," is true if and only if there are more existentialist philosophers in Paris, France, than in Paris, Texas.[2]

The understanding of truth as *a statement that corresponds with reality* is straightforward and accords well with common sense and common usage for the word *true*. Consider a world-renowned philosopher of truth on her way to deliver a lecture at a university theater. After becoming lost, she approaches two students and tentatively asks them: "Is it true that the theater is behind this parking garage?" While this great philosopher might have written hundreds of highly technical pages on the concept of truth, nonetheless, in this unguarded moment she is concerned with truth in the basic way described by Aristotle and most people in the street. That is, she wants to know that her statement correctly describes (or corresponds to) reality. In other words, she wants to know whether the theater is *in fact* behind the parking garage.

I believe that correspondence truth is fundamentally correct so far as it goes (more on that "so far as it goes" qualification momentarily). That is, I believe that a statement is true if and only if it correctly

---

1. Cited in Carl G. Vaught, "Metaphor, Analogy, and the Nature of Truth," *New Essays in Metaphysics,* ed. Robert C. Neville (Albany, NY: SUNY Press, 1987), 218.
2. I have discussed the issue at more length in *Theology in Search of Foundations* (Oxford: Oxford University Press, 2009), chapter 4.

describes reality. It is important that we begin with common agreement on this point since this basic correspondence understanding of truth, as obvious as it may seem, has come under attack in recent decades. A number of people have charged that correspondence is uninformative or even meaningless. However, neither of these charges seems to me to be plausible. Others have warned that a correspondence understanding of truth will lead to a general skepticism (the view that we cannot know anything about the world), but in my opinion the problem here lies not with correspondence truth but rather with a person's theory of knowledge. In sum, none of these objections are especially convincing.

The other major way to argue against correspondence is by proposing another more plausible theory of truth. For instance, some people have argued that truth should be understood to consist in consensus: that is, truth is what everybody agrees with. Another popular suggestion is that truth is really a pragmatic concept: put bluntly, truth is what works. But such suggestions have things backward. The statement that "there are more existentialist philosophers in Paris, France, than in Paris, Texas," is not true because most everybody agrees with it. Rather, most everybody agrees with it because it is true. And the statement "the theater is behind the parking garage" is not true because it is pragmatically useful to direct me to the theater. Rather, it is pragmatically useful to direct me to the theater because it is true. In each case correspondence is always more likely an explanation of truth than the competing theories. Indeed, a little reflection shows that noncorrespondence theories, like consensus and pragmatism, depend implicitly on the correspondence notion of truth. For instance, people who argue that truth is what works do not think that the statement "truth is what works" is itself true because it works. Rather, they believe that this statement accurately describes (or corresponds to) the nature of truth.[3] Thus, try as some may, we cannot get away from correspondence.

As implausible as noncorrespondence conceptions of truth may be, these views have impacted the church in several subtle ways. For instance, consider that many evangelicals hold to a method of small-group Bible study that implies a sort of consensus approach to truth. English writer Harry Blamires observed the rise of this trend in England fifty years ago:

> I have known educated people, professing Christians, who purposely gathered together for religious discussion men and women representing the widest possible varieties of religious conviction. This was fair enough. But unfortunately their aim, as they put it, was to get everyone to make his "individual contribution" (how fraught with error this phrase can be) so that collectively they might arrive at the truth. Now there is much to be said, socially and intellectually, for bringing together people of different outlooks and beliefs; but there is no rational basis for the notion that by mixing a number of conflicting views you are likely to arrive at the truth. You cannot construct truth from a mass of dissonant and disparate material. You cannot *construct* truth at all: you can only *discover* it. And the more noisily opinionated people intervene with their contributions, the less likely you are to discover it.[4]

---

3. William Lane Craig and J. P. Moreland observed that "those who reject the correspondence theory either take their own utterances to be true in the correspondence sense or they do not. If the former, then those utterances are self-defeating. If the latter, there is no reason to accept them, because one cannot take their utterances to be true." *Philosophical Foundations for a Christian Worldview* (Downers Grove, IL: InterVarsity Press, 2003), 140.

4. Blamires, *The Christian Mind* (London: SPCK, 1963), 112.

In my experience many small groups in North America today evince a similar method of studying the Bible: that is, they proceed around the room and pool opinions on the text. Typically in groups like this the leader's role consists of little more than asking each person, "What does this passage mean to you?" with no attempt to discern the objective meaning of the text. Blamires responded to this disturbing trend by affirming the objective status of truth: "Truth is more like a rock than a pudding—a rock which you lay bare by scraping away the soil."[5] We too need to fight against noncorrespondence conceptions of truth.

At this point, the only remaining reason a Christian might have to reject correspondence is if it contradicts Scripture. But, on the contrary, a quick look supports the conclusion that, far from rejecting correspondence, Scripture actually *assumes* it. To begin with, we can consider Joseph's words to his brothers after they came to Egypt, seeking grain for their family. Prior to revealing his identity as their long-lost sibling, Joseph resolved to keep all but one of his brothers in prison "so that your words may be tested to see if you are telling the truth" (Genesis 42:16). In short, Joseph was testing them to ensure that their testimony of their circumstances accurately represented reality. There are many other places in Scripture where the correspondence understanding of truth is assumed. For instance, we read in 1 John 1:8: "If we claim to be without sin, we deceive ourselves and the truth is not in us." Here John was clearly assuming that the standard of truth is a statement that reflects reality; since the claim that we are without sin does not reflect reality, it is not true.[6]

Now back to the "so far as it goes" qualification. While Scripture assumes correspondence truth, I believe it also goes beyond it. Our starting motivation for going beyond correspondence comes from the

---

5. Blamires, *The Christian Mind,* 113.

6. Many other biblical texts assume a correspondence view of truth including 1 Kings 17:24; Psalm 119:43; and Proverbs 12:17.

fact that Scripture makes statements that apply truth not only to statements but also to *persons*. The most important example is when Jesus declared, "I am the way and the truth and the life" (John 14:6). The context of the passage is Jesus's promise that he was going to prepare a place for his disciples. This prompted Thomas to ask how they would find their way to that place, to which Jesus replied that *he* is the way, the truth, and the life. In other words, Jesus came not simply to communicate a series of true statements about how to be set free (as had many religious teachers before him). More importantly, he came as *the* way, truth and life. And so when Philip then asked Jesus to reveal the Father, Jesus replied, "Don't you know me, Philip, even after I have been among you such a long time? *Anyone who has seen me has seen the Father*" (John 14:9, emphasis added). As the personal truth of God, Jesus reflected in his very being the truth of the Father infinitely more fully than any theology textbook ever could. Just as a statement that reflects reality accurately is the truth of what it describes, so Christ, as the perfect reflection of God, is the truth of God. It is with good reason that the AD 325 Creed of Nicaea declares Jesus to be "true God of true God." But that is not all. In addition to being the truth of God, Jesus also represents the truth of perfect humanity. To see the paradigm example of a human being, we ought to look not to Adam but to Christ. Thus, our destiny as glorified human beings is to become like Christ (Romans 8:29), the one person who represents the truth of God and humanity.

If Jesus is the truth, then clearly the truth does not apply only to statements. The fact that Jesus is the truth of divine and human being prompts us to expand our notion of truth. In short, it forces us to recognize that truth can apply to more than just statements. Philosopher Nicholas Wolterstorff provided us with a useful way to expand our thinking about truth when he argued that the core relation of truth is found in the quality of "measuring up in being or excellence." Certainly, this quality applies to statements such that a true statement is one that measures up to the facts. A true sentence is an example of linguistic or propositional truth. But there are other types of truth as well. As Wolterstorff explained, "When we speak of 'a true so-and-so,' we are implicitly measuring a contrast between this so-and-so that measures up and other so-and-so's that do not, or would not, measure up."[7] While a true statement is one that measures up to the facts, many other things can measure up to objective standards as well. For instance, as Wolterstorff explained, a true cup of coffee is one that measures up to the qualities of coffee perfection, while a true friend is one who measures up to the qualities of perfect friendship.

In this sense any entity can be more or less true, depending on how well it matches up to the standard of perfection for the type of thing that it is. While statements measure up if they accurately describe reality, many other things can measure up more or less relative to their natures; and to the extent that they do, they are true. And it all starts with Jesus, for there is no higher reality than God and thus no more important truth than Jesus, who is the perfect reflection of God: he alone measures up perfectly to God. This has great significance for fallen human persons like you and me. We were uniquely made in the image of God, a fact that suggests that the truth of human personhood is found in the extent to which we faithfully image that identity. But equally importantly, we are to be conformed to the image of him who is himself the image of God, Jesus Christ. Thus, we become the truth only insofar as we conform to Christ.

As a result, just as our statements can be true, so can our persons, although the measuring up is different in both cases. The psalmist prayed to the Lord, "Guide me in your truth" (Psalm 25:5), and John observed that we are called to walk in the truth (2 John 1:4). When we understand that the fullest revelation of the truth of God is found in Jesus, we realize that we are praying to be conformed to

---

7. Wolterstorff, "True Words," *But Is It All True? The Bible and the Question of Truth,* ed. Alan G. Padgett and Patrick R. Keifert (Grand Rapids, MI, and Cambridge: Eerdmans, 2006), 42.

the truthful image of God's Son. This means that being faithful to the truth is about much more than believing a particular set of statements that happen to describe reality accurately. When we fail to see the all-encompassing, character-forming nature of truth—the call to be like Christ in all things—we become poor witnesses to truth.

Fightin' for Truth?

So far we have seen that it is important not only to know a set of truths but also to be people of truth. In light of this we must ask what a person characterized by truth looks like. One of the most difficult questions for us concerns how we find people who are passionate about the truth. What do such people formed by truth look like? A moment's reflection on Jesus suggests some obvious characteristics. First, passion: Jesus obviously had passion for the truth, and so should we. Second, conviction: Jesus knew exactly what he believed, so he didn't speak with the voice of doubt but rather with certainty. He knew exactly who he was. Finally, simplicity or clarity: Jesus was not wishy-washy about the truth but rather laid it out as clear as day. For instance, with a striking lack of qualification Jesus spoke God's judgment to the Pharisees: "Woe to you, because you are like unmarked graves, which people walk over without knowing it" (Luke 11:44). So if we want this same kind of love for truth, we too need this deep passion about the truth, an unshakable conviction about the truth, and a simple clarity for how that truth is to be understood.

There is surely much to commend in this analysis. But even so, it seems to me that it is dangerously incomplete. While it is true that Jesus had an undeniable passion, conviction, and simplicity in his grasp of the truth, we must always keep in mind that we are not Jesus. While his passions were singularly submitted to the Father, ours rarely are. And while his conviction was rooted in a sure knowledge of his own identity and call, our convictions are very often mistaken. Finally, Jesus dissected issues precisely because of his correctly-ordered passions and unshakable knowledge. But our simple judgments very often come out of our disordered passions and all-too-fallible convictions. When we lose sight of this and think that mere passion, conviction, and simplicity are enough, our witness to truth inevitably suffers. With this in mind, we will now turn to consider a couple of examples of individuals many see as fitting the bill for a passionate truth seeker. Though they exude the passion, conviction, and simplicity of Jesus, they may lack the subtler virtues of truth that we will analyze in chapters three through six.

We will begin with the dramatic evangelist of the early twentieth century, Billy Sunday. Trained originally as a professional baseball player with the Chicago White Stockings, Billy Sunday converted to Christianity in 1886/7. In 1891 he left baseball to work for the Chicago YMCA; soon after, under the tutelage of evangelist J. Wilbur Chapman, this uneducated athlete was preaching in front of growing crowds. Apparently it didn't matter that he had no formal biblical training (or even a high school diploma), for his boundless energy, dramatic presence, and vocal concern for the truth more than made up for his lack of education. Sunday was passionate about the truth. H. L. Mencken, who spent several nights attending Sunday's revival meetings, captured the preacher's frenetic energy when he wrote: "Sunday tells the simplest anecdote with the triumphant yelp of Satan sighting another archbishop in the chute."[8] It was this kind of conviction, passion, and simplicity that resonated deeply with a large segment of the public and convinced it that Sunday was a man of truth. He certainly had the unshakable conviction, passion, and simple, black-and-white categories (e.g., good and evil, right and wrong, God and the Devil) that many have associated with a serious attitude toward truth.

Not surprisingly, Sunday's conviction, passion, and simple vision were commonly expressed in rather bracing, even breathtaking

---

8. Mencken, "A Day with Billy Sunday," *H .L. Mencken on Religion,* ed. S. T. Joshi (Amherst, NY: Prometheus Books, 2002), 119.

treatments (we might call them annihilations) of his various opponents. A fine example is found in Sunday's dismissive treatment of "liberal scholarship." Rather than engage liberal scholars with a careful and nuanced analysis, he brashly proclaimed: "When the word of God says one thing and scholarship says another, scholarship can go to hell."[9] As Roger Bruns put it,

> For Billy, the egghead philosophers challenging his Bible were just other enemies to smite. The Christian life, the revivalist preached, was always a struggle to preserve basic, fundamental values. The slackers and trimmers, the skeptic and philosophers attacking the truths of the Bible were all agents of the devil. They should not be dealt with through reason or compromise but must be pummelled.[10]

Pummel them he did, although with a flurry of salty verbs and spicy adjectives rather than white-knuckled fists. People loved Sunday because they believed in him. And they believed in his passion, conviction, and the simplicity that enabled him to smite dissent.

As I have suggested, this way of identifying the seeker of truth—that is, by looking for blinding passion, unshakable conviction, and a simple clarity—is enormously tempting. It is like shopping for a restaurant by seeking the most caloric bang for your buck. Unfortunately, even if this method has its attractions, it is a very poor way to choose a nourishing meal: fast food may load you up with calories, but it offers very little by way of nourishing content. And so it is often for those who trumpet truth but have no appreciation for their own limitations of vision or fallibility, let alone the complexity of

---

9. Cited in Heather Hendershot, *Shaking the World for Jesus: Media and Conservative Evangelical Culture* (Chicago: University of Chicago Press, 2004), 172.
10. Roger A. Bruns, *Preacher: Billy Sunday and Big-Time American Evangelism* (New York: W.W. Norton, 1992), 120.

the issues they address. Take in a Billy Sunday sermon, and you would get loaded up on a high caloric count of passion, conviction, and refreshing simplicity, but you would find a disappointingly low level of cognitive nutrition. In order to find a worthwhile meal, you cannot limit your criteria to the cheapest price and highest calorie count, for this is not sufficient for the body or mind. In the same way, when we are seeking truth, we cannot allow ourselves to be persuaded simply by passion, conviction, and simplicity. The truthful person just may be the one whose passion is subtle, whose conviction is understated, and whose appreciation for clarity comes nuanced in qualifications that are necessary to capture an often messy reality.

I believe much of the truth passion that is currently gripping evangelicals (as captured in the many books referenced in chapter one) is but more of that Billy Sunday spirit that quashes critical distance, doubt, and complexity by silencing it with passion, conviction, and simplicity. It is important to appreciate that the spirit of truth is found not merely in the fundamentalist preacher who delivers his exhortations with a steady shower of spittle on the unfortunate first three rows of his flock. The passion, conviction, and distorting pursuit of clarity can come with a much greater degree of sophistication than Billy Sunday ever imagined.

With that we can turn to our second example, a resource that has of late gotten many evangelicals like Ted really excited: *Focus on the Family's The Truth Project*®.[11] In chapter one I described *The Truth Project* as a watershed curriculum, and for good reason. It consists of a complete thirteen-hour worldview curriculum hosted by Del Tackett (former head of the Focus on the Family Institute), and it cost over two million dollars to produce.[12] Mind you, on the surface there is

---

11. All quotes of Del Tackett within this book are drawn from *The Truth Project*, Focus on the Family, 2006.
12. See "Dr. Dobson Introduces The Truth Project," at http://www.thetruthproject.org/about/culturefocus/A000000118.cfm/.

little similarity between Billy Sunday and Del Tackett. While Sunday freely lampooned scholarship, Tackett speaks with a polished, calm, and reassuring tone of measured intensity, unshakable conviction, and intellectual authority. And while Billy Sunday's fundamentalist crusades were marked by a large tent, a crude plywood pulpit, and sawdust floor, Del Tackett's stylish classroom exudes Ivy League appeal, replete with heavy oak desks and brass study lamps. Clearly the ethos is meant to be one of serious academic integrity and unfettered inquiry.

Although the differences between Billy Sunday's revivals and Del Tackett's *The Truth Project* are important, significant pedagogical parallels remain. While Tackett may not wear his passion on his sleeve quite like Sunday, it is undoubtedly present, as is that same unmistakable and unshakable conviction in the rightness of his cause. As I noted above, these characteristics are not in themselves problematic (indeed, they are present, and admirably so, in Jesus). What is problematic is a clearness of vision that comes at the expense of appropriate nuance and self-criticism, and it is here that I must take issue with Tackett's presentation in *The Truth Project*.[13] Here's an example: Tackett may not agree with Sunday that impious scholarship can "go to hell," but he nonetheless provided his own inexcusably sweeping dismissal of

---

13. Given the scope of *The Truth Project* and some of the strong feelings about it, I should give some of my background with it. I first came across *The Truth Project* when it came out in 2006. I initially viewed one of the sessions with the hope that I could use it to supplement an adult Sunday school class I was teaching on Christian Worldview. While I was very disappointed and opted not to use it, I resolved to watch the entire curriculum with the possibility of developing a critical response to it. And so in February 2007 I sat down and watched all thirteen hours while taking careful notes. I presented my findings at the Evangelical Theological Society (San Diego, 2007) and was warmly received by the audience of academics, many of whom were familiar with the curriculum and shared my concerns about it. A month later (December 2007) I completed a journal article critiquing the curriculum. Before sending it out for review I emailed Focus asking if they would like a copy so they could offer a response before I sent it for publication. I received no reply so I sent it to Christian Scholar's Review, and they accepted it for publication. See "Learning in a Time of (Cultural) War: Indoctrination in Focus on the Family's *The Truth Project*™," 39 (2009).

the academy. The context is the tenth session of the curriculum when Tackett turned to discuss the United States. In the session Tackett complained that "it is in vogue today to hate America." He added that "there is a deep hatred of America within liberal academia." Tackett did not explain what he meant by "liberal academia," but I get the sense that it consists of large swaths of the faculties at most public universities. This already is a comment of staggering scope: How could he possibly defend the claim that a large section of the academic establishment in American higher education literally *hates* the nation it lives and teaches in? The sheer unqualified nature of the claim should startle the viewer. But things get even more incredible, for Tackett then claimed that the hatred that some liberal academics have for America derives from the declaration of the New England Confederation of 1643 "to advance the kingdome of our Lord Jesus Christ." Tackett then explained: "That's why they came, and I think that it is because of that foundation, it is because of those roots, that we see that it is now in vogue to hate America."

Let's consider whether there is any evidence for Tackett's rather startling claim. In order to test Tackett's claim, consider one of the most widely recognized publications of recent "liberal" academic scholarship, historian Howard Zinn's best-selling work (1.5 million copies in print) of revisionary history, *A People's History of the United States*.[14] Zinn recognized that history has often been told by the winners, and so he sought to retell the history of the United States from the perspective of the oppressed underclasses. (While this is a common exercise today, Zinn was breaking new ground three decades ago.) And so, beginning with the horrific genocides under the sixteenth-century conquistadors, Zinn narrated an oft-overlooked history. Could Tackett seriously claim that by undertaking this project Howard Zinn was evincing a deep-seated hostility to the seventeenth-century

---

14. (New York: Harper and Row, 1980).

Pilgrims? On the contrary, by Zinn retelling this history in the hopes of establishing a more just and equitable society, we could argue that he was, in point of fact, fighting for the poor and oppressed in a way that echoes and anticipates the kingdom of our Lord Jesus Christ. A person may not agree with Zinn's analysis, but surely to dismiss it (and much of the rest of contemporary scholarship) as anti-Christian polemic is absolutely indefensible.

While Ted is skeptical of the kind of fundamentalism represented by Billy Sunday, he finds in the more measured and sophisticated tone of Del Tackett a partner in the truth. Tackett never yells, and he certainly doesn't dance on stage like Billy Sunday. Nor does he avail himself of Sunday's rather colorful vocabulary (particularly concerning the fate of the Devil). And Ted is duly attracted to what seems to be a deepened sophistication evident in Del Tackett over that of Billy Sunday. However, I would submit that these differences are largely cosmetic. A closer look reveals that Tackett shares Billy Sunday's passion, conviction, and simplicity.

Truth at War

What happens when people are taken in by the notion that a truthful person is simply one who exudes passion, conviction, and simplicity? As I have said, the problem with this vision is not that it is wrong, but rather that it is dangerously incomplete. The greatest danger arising from this incomplete vision is pragmatism. Mind you, we are no longer speaking here about the pragmatism that offers a formal redefinition of truth as whatever works, but rather the default kind that we fall into when we are more concerned with defending our beliefs than ensuring that they are in fact true.

Let's begin here with a simple example. Given that Christians are called to be people of the truth, we would expect that the church pulpit would be the one place in society where truth statements would be most rigorously analyzed and vetted. But alas, in my experience, the pulpit is often the first place where the call for truth collapses into the siren song of pragmatism. Just consider the proliferation of urban legends in the pulpit.[15] For instance, I have heard the following story used as a sermon illustration in churches on separate occasions. It concerns the case of the missionary who returned to report at his home church in Michigan. In the service he told them that he had been traveling through the jungle in Africa alone when a young man came up to him. This young man informed the missionary that his gang had been planning on robbing the missionary the previous night when he was camping alone in the woods. But they called off the attack when they came upon his campsite and saw him surrounded by twenty-six burly bodyguards. Given that he was traveling alone, the missionary was stunned at this testimony. At that moment in the story, a man from the Michigan church stood up and asked the missionary on which day this had happened. When the missionary told him, the church realized that it was the same day that twenty-six of them had gathered to pray for the missionary's safety. A miracle!

The story is obviously well intentioned as an illustration of the power of prayer according to James 5:16. But that good intention does not change the fact that this is a well-known urban legend with several elements in the story that make it implausible. As the writer on the premier urban legend website www.snopes.com observed of this case: "It's sadly ironic that so many tales contrived to display a particular belief system as The One True Way include fabrications tossed in to better carry the message."[16] Do we really need to resort to urban legends to illustrate the power of prayer? Sadly, this is but one example of the many urban legends that are preached every year from the pulpit. The question is why so many preachers are so quick to use

---

15. For a perceptive discussion of the problem, see John Williams, *The Cost of Deception: The Seduction of Modern Myths and Urban Legends* (Nashville: Broadman & Holman, 2001).

16. For the complete story and an explanation of the implausible elements, see the website http://www.snopes.com/glurge/26guards.asp.

stories that any moderately trained folklorist could spot from a mile away. The answer, I fear, is that often pastors under time constraints are looking for the most effective illustration in the shortest amount of time: sadly, within this pragmatic ethos truth takes the hindmost.

It is important to appreciate how this pragmatic attitude is a natural outgrowth of the fundamentalist spirit of passion, conviction, and simplicity. The progression from fundamentalism to pragmatism is natural, for once we have opted to sacrifice nuance and complexity for the sake of winning the argument, we are prone to fall into the warfare picture of intellectual combat in which winning the argument trumps nuance and complexity. Howard Zinn (our above-mentioned liberal historian) observed: "It seems that once an initial judgment has been made that a war is just, there is a tendency to stop thinking, to assume then that everything done on behalf of victory is morally acceptable."[17] Whether it is a war of tanks and bombs or a heated discussion around the watercooler, once we draw our line in the sand, this same dynamic often takes over.

Clint Eastwood's film *Flags of Our Fathers* provides a particularly memorable, if sober, account of the pragmatism of war. The film (based on the book of the same name) relays the story behind the famous photo of the Iwo Jima flag raising on February 23, 1945. In the iconic image six soldiers are shown struggling to raise the American flag on the peak of Mount Suribachi. As the film unfolds, we see how this was the second flag raising of the day, undertaken precisely for the purpose of posterity. As a result, within hours the picture was distributed around the world and used as a source of national pride in the war bonds campaign. In other words, the actual complex truth of the matter was suppressed to spur on the war effort. Three of the soldiers are then sent back to go on the road for the war bonds campaign. As the campaign progresses, the soldiers repeatedly confront the fact that

---

17. Howard Zinn, "Just and Unjust War," in *Passionate Declarations: Essays on War and Justice* (New York: Harper Collins, 2003), 96.

truths about the war and the United States are concealed for the sake of raising money and winning the war.[18] One of the soldiers summarizes the rationale for repeatedly suppressing truths for the sake of the war bonds campaign: "We need easy to understand truths and damn few words." That could well be the mantra of the truth pragmatist: Don't give me truth in all its complexity and nuance. Give me what I need to win the battle.

So, the pragmatist focuses on passion for the cause, simplicity of the message, and above all the need to defeat the other for the cause of truth. *The Truth Project* provides an echo of the Suribachi wartime photo in its own promotional materials, though here the intent is apparently not to inspire but rather to inculcate fear. The example concerns the following shocking statistic that is cited in the materials from consummate pollster George Barna: only 9 percent of "professing Christians" have a "biblical worldview." The statistic is used to good effect in these materials, presumably to jolt a complacent evangelical public into recognizing the enormous need for this type of curriculum. After all, it does not take a genius to figure out that if *less than one out of ten Christians has a biblical worldview*, then we are in serious trouble indeed.

A closer look at the statistic reveals that just like the Iwo Jima flag-raising photo, it has complications that, if they were fully appreciated, would undermine its value for the purposes for which it was employed. In other words, those who are adequately reflective and concerned with the truth could not avail themselves of this statistic. In order to see this, we can begin by taking a closer look at the 9 percent statistic. Going to Barna's website, we discover that in the survey he defined "biblical worldview" with reference to eight criteria.[19] For a

---

18. Spinning the truth for the war effort is, of course, very common. The 2004 documentary *Control Room* chronicles the way that both Al Jazeera (the Qatar news network) and Western news agencies provided very different coverage of the 2003 US invasion of Iraq, each complaining of the other's propaganda.

19. See "A Biblical Worldview Has a Radical Effect on a Person's Life," at http://www.barna.org/FlexPage.aspx?Page=BarnaUpdate&BarnaUpdateID=154.

person to count as having a biblical worldview, that individual must assent to all eight of Barna's criteria. If they fail to agree with all eight, then by definition they do not have a biblical worldview. This might be okay if the criteria in question were both clear and uncontroversial; unfortunately, a number of Barna's criteria are neither. Consider but one of them, which I'll refer to as the "Bible Criterion," or "BC" for short: "The Bible is the source of absolute moral truth." According to Barna's assumptions, if you do not accept BC, then you do not have a biblical worldview. But in order to decide whether we ought to assent to BC, we presumably must first have an understanding of what it is we are assenting to. Unfortunately, BC is not clear in this regard at all. Indeed, a cursory reading suggests there are at least two possible interpretations: (1) the Bible is the ontological source of all moral truths (that is, they derive their existence from the Bible); or (2) the Bible is the epistemological source of all moral truths (that is, it provides the way that we know them). But alas, both of these claims are indisputably *false.* The Bible is not the source of all moral truths: God is. Nor is the Bible the single way we know moral truths since many moral truths are part of the natural law. (For instance, the commandment to honor one's father and mother is recognized across cultures and religious traditions, as is the Golden Rule.) So, whether or not we interpret BC as an ontological statement (all moral truths are grounded in the Bible) or an epistemological one (we know all moral truths through the Bible), it ought to be rejected.

The same problems that beset BC are faced by a number of Barna's other seven criteria.[20] Indeed, once we have come to appreciate just how problematic the definition is, it may be that the only good news is that a scant 9 percent of respondents found these criteria to be adequate. In other words, from this perspective the 9 percent statistic

---

20. And then there is the fact that Barna's criteria of a biblical worldview do not include basic doctrines that should surely be a part of a biblical worldview, such as the verbal inspiration of Scripture, the Trinity, the incarnation, and substitutionary atonement.

might evince not an unbiblical mind, but rather an encouragingly critical one. Since we cannot know which of these two factors is actually relevant, the best conclusion would seem to be that the statistic is, for all intents and purposes, useless. Though the statistic has no value, it was ironically appropriated for the serious work of persuading a lackadaisical evangelical public of the value of *The Truth Project*. Sadly, this use of statistics is not uncommon. Indeed, sociologist Christian Smith has observed that "American evangelicals, who profess to be committed to Truth, are among the worst abusers of simple descriptive statistics, which claim to represent the truth about reality, of any group I have ever seen."[21]

Coda

When my daughter was five years old, I saw her looking through a Toys "R" Us flier, her eyes sparkling at all the products available for purchase. When she began to point out all the different toys that she would like, I replied: "Toys are great to have, but what is *really* important?" To my delight (and surprise) she replied immediately: "*Truth!*" Then as an afterthought she added: "But board games are okay too." Indeed they are. The world is crowded with many things to which we can commit some well-spent time and effort, board games included. Even so, nothing is more important than truth, both the truth that we know and above all the truth that forms us into being people of truth. But where do we find the aspects of a truthful character if not simply in passion, simplicity, and the convictions of combat? It is to that question that we now turn.

---

21. "Evangelicals Behaving Badly with Statistics," *Books and Culture* (Jan/Feb 2007) available at http://www.christianitytoday.com/bc/2007/001/5.11.html.

3

IF JESUS WERE NOT THE TRUTH, HE'D BE THE **FIRST PERSON** TO TELL YOU TO LOOK ELSEWHERE[1]

The Newbery Medal–winning children's book *The Summer of the Swans* tells the story of one unforgettable day in the life of fourteen-year-old Sara. As she wakes in the morning, she discovers that her ten-year-old mentally challenged brother, Charlie, has gone missing. As word of the boy's disappearance spreads, Sara is approached by schoolmate Joe Melby, who graciously offers to join in the search. But Sara is unimpressed as she believes that Joe stole Charlie's watch some months before. And so rather than graciously accept the offer, she instead accuses Joe of the theft. Joe is shocked to learn of Sara's suspicions, and he replies by explaining why he could not be guilty of the crime. The persuasiveness of Joe's defense catches Sara off guard. For the previous several months she has been telling others that Joe

---

1. The title of this chapter comes from a phrase I first heard from Dallas Willard.

stole the watch, but now that she hears the strength of his reasoned defense, she finds herself no longer as certain of his guilt.

Given the significance of Joe's testimony, we would expect Sara to be especially attentive to it. But instead it is precisely when it is most important for Sara to listen and reflect that she opts to reinforce her original beliefs: "She turned and started walking with great speed down the hill. For some reason she was not as sure about Joe Melby as she had been before, and this was even more disturbing. He did take the watch, she said to herself." [2] Why does Sara opt to retrench in her beliefs at this moment rather than consider Joe's defense? The answer is sobering: "She could not bear to think that she had been mistaken in this, that she had taken revenge on the wrong person."[3] Sadly, it would appear that she is unwilling to consider that she has been terribly wrong about Joe. By walking away, she reveals that she would rather live with a false belief than face a difficult truth.

But this only deepens the mystery. To get a sense of how inexplicable and even bizarre Sara's behavior appears to be, consider the following analogy. Imagine that Ted is driving down the highway toward Denver when he pulls off the road into a filling station for gas. While the attendant is filling his car, she asks Ted where he is headed. After he tells her he is driving toward Denver, she informs him that he is traveling in the wrong direction. With that she pulls out a map and shows Ted that he is traveling north on Highway 25 when he should be going east on Highway 34. Given the credibility of the attendant's testimony, we would expect at the very least that Ted would pull out his own road atlas and carefully reassess before continuing down the highway in what may very well be the completely wrong direction. So imagine if instead he quelled the new doubts that had been raised by the attendant's testimony and sped back onto the highway in the same

---

2. Betsy Byars, *The Summer of the Swans* (New York: Scholastic, 1970), 90.

3. Byars, *The Summer of the Swans*, 90.

direction. Such behavior would be bizarre indeed, as each mile could be leading him farther away from his intended destination. And yet, as bizarre as Ted's action would be, it is really no different from Sara's decision to ignore Joe Melby's testimony.

Before we judge Sara and Ted too harshly, we would do well to recall Jesus' words: "Let any one of you who is without sin be the first to throw a stone at her." (John 8:7). Truth be known, I suspect that we are not as different from Ted and Sara as we might like to think. The fact is that we all struggle with a tendency to defend our beliefs precisely when they are most in need of critical reevaluation. And this behavior suggests that we are often less serious about pursuing the truth than we would like to think. In this chapter we will explore this defensive attitude, known to psychologists as the confirmation bias, which predisposes us to accept evidence that supports our beliefs while dismissing evidence that does not. It is crucial to understand the confirmation bias because it is inimical to a character formed by truth. Once we understand how this trait works, we will consider it from a biblical perspective. Finally, we will consider how Christians often evince a confirmation bias in their treatment of the problem of evil.

What Are the Limits to "the Benefit of the Doubt"?

Some time after nine o'clock in the morning on June 12, 2006, Charla Mack was brutally stabbed to death in her own garage. Later that same morning Judge Chuck Weller, the presiding judge at Mack's divorce hearing, was shot (and wounded) in his chambers by a sniper. All the evidence for both crimes implicated Mack's estranged husband, Darren. Apparently enraged by what he considered to be a grossly unfair divorce settlement, Mack had gone to his wife's house that morning and confronted her in the garage with a large knife. He then repeatedly stabbed her, slit her throat, and left her to die on the concrete floor. Next, Mack, an experienced marksman, traveled downtown and shot the judge in his chambers from across the street.[4] Despite the overwhelming evidence implicating Mack in his wife's murder, he pleaded not guilty, claiming that he killed her out of self-defense. As Mack told it, when he entered the house with a large knife, his intentions were wholly peaceable: it was only when Charla produced a gun (although forensics found no evidence of a gun) that he was forced to butcher her in a desperate struggle to save his own life. Needless to say, it took the jury just a few hours to decide to convict.

As terribly implausible as Mack's defense may have appeared to most rational people, he did retain a handful of faithful supporters, including his brother, son, and a few friends. This modest coterie remained absolutely convinced of Mack's account of the events and thus considered his conviction to be a gross miscarriage of justice. This support is frankly perplexing for the rest of us who will be left to wonder how rational people could look at the evidence and conclude that Mack is anything but guilty. Could it be that Mack's supporters are cognitively deficient and so unable to assess the evidence? Or could they be coconspirators, wickedly attempting to suppress the truth of Mack's guilt? How else could Mack's supporters fail to recognize all the evidence implicating him in the crime? And what is it about Sara that allows her to walk away from Joe Melby? How could Ted continue on down the highway in what might be the wrong direction? Finally, how is it that we too can dismiss evidence against our belief that would draw the attention of any objective observer?

The diagnosis of the problem is provided by contemporary psychology that identifies this common trait operative in each of these cases as the *confirmation bias*. According to Raymond Nickerson the confirmation bias is a "one-sided case-building process" that is characterized by "unwitting selectivity in the acquisition and use

---

4. For more on the case, see http://darren-mack-news.newslib.com/.

of evidence."[5] Darren Mack's supporters were singularly intent on believing in his innocence, and so they screened out all the evidence implying his guilt. Ted was intent on believing that he was driving in the right direction, and so he screened out any evidence to the contrary. And Sara was intent on believing that Joe Melby was guilty, and so she screened out any evidence that would support his innocence.

While the confirmation bias is dangerous if left unchecked, a particular degree of bias in favor of presently accepted beliefs is both natural and proper. For instance, it is appropriate to exercise a degree of bias (though *deference* might be a better word) in favor of people we know. Think of a child who is taken to the doctor's office and subjected to a number of uncomfortable tests with her mother looking on. While the child cannot understand why her mother allows her to be subjected to these unpleasant tests, she trusts that her mother has her best interests in mind. Trusting people we know well, even when some of the evidence appears to go against their character, is an appropriate exercise of the confirmation bias.

Building on this point, I would contend that just as it is appropriate to defer to people we already trust, so it is appropriate to defer to beliefs that we already trust. As a result, it may be appropriate to continue to hold certain beliefs even when some of the evidence goes against them. For instance, a conservative Christian who finds his faith shaken after reading Richard Dawkins's *The God Delusion* may be doing nothing wrong when he retains his Christian belief, even if he as yet has no reply to some of Dawkins's points. He can recognize that his belief system faces some difficulties while still concluding at the end of the day that he throws his lot in with Christianity. Of course the point goes the other way as well. The atheist who finds her faith shaken after reading Scott Hahn and Benjamin Wiker's *Answering the New Atheism* is also doing nothing wrong when she retains her belief

---

5. Raymond S. Nickerson, "Confirmation Bias: A Ubiquitous Phenomenon in Many Guises," *Review of General Psychology* 2, no. 2 (1998): 175.

in atheism despite her inability to rebut all their points. The point is not that we get a free pass to hold our beliefs rationally no matter what the evidence may be against them. Rather, the point is simply that a degree of deference in favor of our presently held beliefs is psychologically natural and rationally defensible.

So it would seem that the problem lies not with the confirmation bias per se but rather with its inappropriate application. We can trust certain persons and beliefs even when certain evidence doesn't jibe with that trust. But that doesn't mean that we can trust them come what may. (The mother who viciously beats her children "for their own good" is no longer acting in a way that still warrants trust.) The real problem is not that we exercise a confirmation bias as if rationality requires us to remain cool and calculating Vulcans. Rather the problem is that we are typically quite resistant to examining our bias. As a result, we often end up letting the confirmation bias run amok.

Keeping an Eye on the Confirmation Bias

Why is it that when a challenge to our beliefs arises, our first inclination is to adopt a defensive posture rather than an open and carefully discerning attitude? Why are we so resistant to examining our own confirmation bias? I would suggest two significant reasons. First, we are often victims of our own intellectual inertia or laziness. In short, it is often simply easier to stay with the status quo than to revise our beliefs. While mere inertia may be understandable, it is far from defensible, especially when the beliefs at issue concern matters of grave significance. The second, and I suspect more significant reason, arises from fear: that is, examination of our confirmation bias means admitting evidence that challenges our beliefs, and this process can be very unsettling.

Consider again the moment when Sara is confronted with Joe's innocence: "*She could not bear to think that she had been mistaken.*" Unable to contemplate the thought that she has wronged Joe, Sara opts instead to shut out his claims by attacking instead of apologizing. Similarly, Mack's supporters seem unable to consider that their father, son, or friend could possibly be guilty of such a heinous crime, and so they cope by ignoring the evidence and blaming the victim. For a vivid illustration of fear, I recall another trial where two children were implicated in conspiracy to murder their own parents. Although the children were convicted in part by an FBI recording of them laying out their plan, the parents continued to insist that their children were innocent, all the while resolutely refusing even to listen to the recording. That reaction can be understood only as fear, a sheer inability to confront an admittedly terrible truth.

Sadly, Christians would seem to be as susceptible to the fear factor as anybody else. I recall an instance where a former student of mine was teaching adult Sunday school. When she asked the class members whether they would be interested in studying the historical evidence for the life, death, and resurrection of Jesus, one woman strongly objected. The reason? She knew of two young men who had gone to universities to study the historical evidence for Jesus and had lost their faith as a result. While I would certainly count that a tragedy, note the moral she drew from the story. It was *not* "stay away from the university," which I could perhaps have understood. Rather, her lesson was "stay away from the history," which I could not understand at all. If the objective historical record does not support Christian claims about Christ, then shouldn't Christians be the first to want to know? Like those parents refusing to listen to their own children's murder plot, this woman demonstrated an indefensible instance of the fear factor.

That woman's refusal to confront the objective historical record conforms with widespread secular assumptions that Christian faith is motivated by insular irrationality. Rather than react to such assumptions defensively, we should use this as an occasion to ask whether there is something about Christianity in particular that encourages the unrestricted reign of our confirmation bias. On the contrary, I believe that when Scripture is properly understood it actually equips us to rein in our confirmation biases. In order to argue the point I will focus on the crucial scriptural emphasis on self-examination. As this theme makes clear, while we are saved by grace and not works, *that does not guarantee us an infallible insight into whether we are true disciples to begin with.* As Paul warned the Corinthians: "Examine yourselves to see whether you are in the faith; test yourselves. Do you not realize that Christ Jesus is in you—unless, of course, you fail the test?" (2 Corinthians 13:5). Paul was well aware of the common human tendency to give ourselves a passing grade in terms of spiritual health (as in other things). As a result, he saw it was much more important to evaluate ourselves carefully, challenging our own innate tendency to give ourselves the benefit of the doubt. The urgency of careful self-examination is evident in sobering form in Jesus' parable of the sheep and goats (Matthew 25:31–46). When those that are goats discover their real identity, it becomes immediately clear that *they thought they were sheep.* That is, they thought they had acted like true disciples. "Lord, when did we see you hungry or thirsty or a stranger or needing clothes or sick or in prison, and did not help you?" (v. 44). This implies that they had convinced themselves that they *were* meeting the needs of those who were hungry, thirsty, a stranger, unclothed, sick, and in prison, even when they clearly were not. This kind of sobering self-deception traces back to the seminal moments when these goats failed to challenge their own confirmation bias. These poor goats carefully noted all the (meager) evidence that supported their standing as sheep, while discounting all the more substantial evidence for their true status as goats.[6]

Every Christian needs to consider his or her confirmation bias in order to determine whether the evidence really supports the conclusion

---

6. Here's an example. While the average evangelical will see him- or herself as minimally generous, average tithing rates among American evangelicals of 3 to 3.5 percent suggest otherwise.

that he or she is a follower of Christ. In light of our heady penchant for self-deception, we always need to consider this question carefully. When we introspect rigorously with a singular desire to see the truth, we are emulating the truthfulness of Christ, who was the one person in history who, I would propose, had no confirmation bias, because of his full submission to the will of his Father. While we can never in this life completely eliminate our confirmation bias any more than we can completely stop sinning, we can always strive to keep it in check by seeking out and renouncing unjustifiable biases in our relentless pursuit of the truth. As a result, we must eschew the reflexive defensive posture when we are under attack and train ourselves instead to listen and assess carefully. If the evidence suggests that in a given matter we do not have the truth, we need to admit it.

Interestingly, if Christians were consistent in affirming the truth and the best arguments wherever they were to be found (even when they went against our beliefs), I suspect it would increase the attractiveness and plausibility of Christian beliefs for others. I am reminded here of Santa Claus (aka Kris Kringle) in the classic film *Miracle on 34th Street*. Although Mr. Kringle took a job as a Macy's store Santa, he never let that stop him from directing shoppers to the best price, even if it was to be found at Macy's archrival Gimbels. This procedure rode roughshod over the legendary archrivalry between these two retail institutions as captured in the once-popular saying "Would Macy's tell Gimbels?" Common sense would suggest that this kind of honesty would have hurt Macy's bottom line, but ironically it had the opposite effect. Even if customers did go elsewhere for a single item, Kringle's honest advice ultimately made them more faithful Macy's customers than they had been before. And perhaps this is not that surprising after all, for Kringle's actions established trust: any business willing to send the customer elsewhere is a trustworthy retailer worthy of faithful patronage. If Christians demonstrated a similar attitude, I suspect that we too would likely become increasingly trusted witnesses to truth.

The confirmation bias is especially problematic when intellectual engagement with others descends to the level of trite caricature, as it so often does. As Nickerson observed, "If one is constantly urged to present reasons for opinions that one holds and is not encouraged also to articulate reasons that could be given against them, one is being trained to exercise a confirmation bias."[7] It follows that if we are serious about the truth, then we will become our own fiercest (and fairest) critic. So what's a good way to go about this? For some guidance here I propose that we consider a method of dialogue common among medieval Scholastic theologians called the Scholastic method. In this method you begin by stating the views of your opponent as powerfully as possible. Only then do you proceed to offer an alternative view, first by systematically deconstructing the case that you have just made and then erecting arguments to support your view. Of course, you shoulder a risk with this method, for you just might present the alternative view so winsomely that you find yourself changing your views. But if your goal is gaining truth rather than simply vindicating present opinions, that shouldn't be a great concern. And what a way to be converted—through *self-persuasion*!

On this point I have often been impressed by the intellectual courage and honesty of people who managed to argue themselves out of one position and into another simply by assessing the data as honestly as possible. In this process we always need to remind ourselves that our abiding goal should not be with protecting our convictions but rather with maximizing the truth. We would do well to follow the spirit, if not necessarily the letter, of the Scholastic method. With that in mind we will now consider the problem of evil. As we do so, we will observe how Christians often try to minimize the problem in a way that skirts its full force.

---

7. Nickerson, "Confirmation Bias: A Ubiquitous Phenomenon in Many Guises," 205.

A Loving God in a World of Evil

At this point we will turn to consider one example of how Christians often play to the confirmation bias. Our topic will be what is, without a doubt, the most painful and difficult topic for Christian faith: the problem of evil. While the rigorous pursuit of truth obliges us to wrestle honestly with the problem of evil, the confirmation bias does its best to downplay the problem. When we refuse to admit the depth of the problem of evil, we do our faith no favors but instead frustrate the formation of our own truthful character.

The core problem at issue concerns how a loving God could allow the kind of heinous evils that we find occurring in the world every day. In my experience, Christian leaders, including pastors, teachers, and apologists, frequently fail to acknowledge the depth of the problem of evil. For a simple example consider the music at the service of a typical evangelical church. The service begins with a number of upbeat songs celebrating the goodness and faithfulness of God. Then it gradually moves into slower, more reflective songs of spiritual devotion and longing. While these emotions are important, few if any of the songs touch on a vast array of emotions that people in the pew wrestle with on a daily basis, including anger, doubt, disappointment, fear, pain, and sadness. What is more, this limited selection of themes creates a distorted, even disingenuous, picture of the individual and corporate Christian life. (Incidentally, it is significant that many of the emotions and thoughts that are subtly excluded by this common form of corporate worship are precisely those that are valuable at examining the confirmation bias.)

The imbalance present in many instances of corporate worship reflects deeper difficulties the church has with addressing the problem of evil and suffering. Just as corporate worship often provides a skewed picture of the problem of evil, so do many formal Christian treatments of evil. Consider again an example drawn from Del Tackett's treatment of the problem of evil in *The Truth Project*. As he turned to address the problem in session three, Tackett reflected the typical confidence of the apologist. As he put it, the existence of evil in the world is a puzzle that "really should be presented back to the world, not to us. We really do have a lot of answers for the issue of evil. The world does not." Tackett went on to expand the point: "Do you understand this question that is constantly laid upon us? The question of evil? And it is usually asked of us in somewhat of a smug way, and I don't mean to be trite about it, but a smug way that implies that not only has the questioner stumped you as a believer but they have somehow toppled Christianity, when in reality we have a lot of answers for this question, and the truth is they have none."

So according to Tackett, while atheists struggle to explain the problem of evil, the Christian has no such problem. This confident approach to evil is common among many Christian pastors, teachers, and apologists who are anxious to defuse the problem and its potentially corrosive impact on faith as quickly as possible. While I agree with the essence of Tackett's response—that is, I believe that the fullest answer to the problem of evil comes from within a Christian context—that does not mean that the Christian answer is completely satisfying intellectually or pastorally. Still less does it mean that we may claim to "have a lot of answers for this question" while "they have none." What is more, I suspect that a more honest confrontation with the wrenching depth of the problem would only increase the credibility of the Christian witness for those in the midst of suffering.

The first evidence that the standard Christian treatment of evil is not completely satisfactory is found in the fact that Christians typically chafe against its implications. In order to see this, we first need to make clear the essence of the mainstream Christian view of providence. The standard account claims that God has perfect control over all events. This entails that he could prevent any evil event from occurring. However, he allows them to occur, and the proposed reason is because he intends to achieve a greater good by doing so. But we are often very uncomfortable about drawing on this greater goods account when people are in the throes of suffering. In fact, when a terrible event happens, well-meaning Christians will often shy away from God's purposeful control of evil altogether by saying things like this: "God didn't *plan* for that tornado to hit your house" or "There's no *reason* why your child has cancer." These statements are hardly surprising, for just imagine how cruel it would be to inform somebody that God *did* plan for that tornado to demolish his or her house, meticulously plotting the disturbance of each blade of grass on the tornado's approach, as well as the trajectory of each piece of shrapnel as the house was torn apart. And who would dare say that God *did* have a good reason for having their child afflicted with cancer, carefully planning the progression of the disease through each cell of the child's body? Many would consider such statements to range somewhere between insensitive and positively monstrous. Surely, only the most inept or callous comforter would offer such abhorrent analyses of these terrible events.

But even if such statements strike us as pastorally insensitive (at best) and downright blasphemous (at worst), according to the standard view of God's providence, they are nonetheless theologically correct. According to that standard view, God has control over every event in creation down to the position of every sparrow and every hair on our heads (Matthew 10:29–31; Luke 12:6–7). It follows from this account that if God allows an evil event, then he does so not out of wickedness or incompetence, but because he knows that it will eventually bring about a compensating good. Once we accept this, it follows that every house destroyed in an extreme weather event and every cancerous tumor that infects a child is part of God's *good plan* that he had decreed for *good reasons*. So when the Jews were speculating on why a particular man was born blind, Jesus could explain that it was "so that the works of God might be displayed in him" (John 9:3). And in Romans 8:28 we read that God uses everything that befalls those called by him for the good, and that would presumably include the destruction of a home and the diagnosis of cancer.

While Christians may be squeamish about affirming God's complete sovereign control over terrible events, Scripture clearly is not. Consider the book of Lamentations, which provides a meditation on the utter hopelessness and incomprehension following the fall of Jerusalem to the Babylonians in 586 BC. The writer described the desperate situation with excruciating detail, observing that priests and prophets were butchered in the sanctuary and that starving women were so desperate that they resorted to eating their own children (2:20). And yet, as horrific as all this was, the writer did not simply pawn off the tragedy on the Babylonians (as we might do today). Rather, he affirmed without apology that *God* acted like an enemy by swallowing up Israel and completely destroying the city (2:5–6). The fact that the judgment came through the Babylonians is, in a certain respect, a mere incidental detail. The bottom line is that the fall of Jerusalem was part of the divine plan:

> The LORD has done what he planned;
>> he has fulfilled his word,
>> which he decreed long ago.
> He has overthrown you without pity,
>> he has let the enemy gloat over you,
>> he has exalted the horn of your foes. (2:17)

The implications of this passage are startling. God foreordained every detail of the destruction of Jerusalem down to the slaughter of priests and cannibalization of children. When was the last time you heard a sermon that probed the depths of anguish in Lamentations, let alone that dared to draw a connection between God's perfect sovereign control in ancient horrors and their contemporary counterparts (Nazi Germany, Rwanda . . .)? If Scripture can attribute the greatest horrors to God's eternal decree without a blush, why don't we?

So to sum up, the first step in challenging our confirmation bias on the problem of evil is found in conceding this tension between theological affirmation and pastoral appropriateness. Traditional views of providence oblige us to accept the fall of Jerusalem, the slaughter of priests, and even the cannibalization of children as in some sense planned providentially by God for certain good. And yet our pastoral wisdom recoils from this very claim pressed on us by orthodox views of providence.

We now have a solid preliminary sense of where the confirmation bias is operative when it comes to concealing tension concerning the problem of evil. But rather than retreat from the terrible terrain, let's linger here awhile longer by contemplating one familiar passage of Scripture, not through the eyes of the comforted but rather through the eyes of the suffering. The verse is Psalm 139:16: "Your eyes saw my unformed body. All the days ordained for me were written in your book before one of them came to be." Encapsulated in this passage is the promise of God's perfect foreknowledge and sovereign control over every event in our lives. Many Christians take comfort in this verse with its description of providential care over individuals long before they were born or even conceived. But do all Christians take comfort in this passage? How does the passage look when we consider it in light of a truly horrifying event? With that question in the background, let's turn to the tragic attempted murder of Carmina Salcido.

On April 15, 1989, Ramon Salcido took his three daughters—Teresa, age two; Carmina, age three; and Sofia, age four—out to a field. He then proceeded with horrifyingly methodic calculation to take each child over his knee, pull back her head, and slit her throat. Here is the account provided by Carmina (the sole survivor): "[He] grabs my hair, pulls my head back and I put my hands up . . . protecting, so he cut open my fingers and I moved them. . . . I move my hands out of the way, [in] one clean cut. It was just like a razor."[8] And there he left them to die, lying facedown in the dirt, with gaping

8. http://abcnews.go.com/2020/carmina-salcido-confronts-dad-left-dead/story?id=8835209.

wounds from ear to ear.[9] Approximately thirty-six hours later the children were found. And while Teresa and Sofia were long since dead, incredibly three-year-old Carmina was still holding on to life.[10]

Undoubtedly, Christians are most successful at dealing with the problem of evil when they treat evil as some abstract quantity that can be isolated and analyzed apart from actual evil events. Kept at the level of abstraction the problem of evil is relatively manageable. As we have seen, God allows evil because of his intent to achieve commensurately greater goods, a view that is called the *greater goods theodicy*.[11] In much the same way that a parent subjects a child to the suffering of chemotherapy to achieve the greater good of a cancer-free body, so God subjects human beings to many horrible experiences, in part, for the greater good of sanctified creatures.

While this theodicy works fine in the abstract (that is, when our discussion is restricted to "evil" and "good" as general qualities abstracted from their concrete instantiations), when applied in the concrete it loses much of its appeal. Indeed, in the minds of some it makes God look positively monstrous. Even for the Christian who accepts God's providential hand working sovereignly in all events, there is something distinctly unpalatable about the notion that an Israelite mother cannibalized her child or a father slit his children's throats so that God might achieve a commensurately greater good. As a result, though I may believe the argument to be valid, I can nonetheless understand why atheists like Richard Dawkins find the reasoning of greater goods theodicy to be "grotesque."[12]

---

9. From that point Salcido returned to the house and killed his wife. He then killed his wife's mother, his two sisters-in-law (ages twelve and eight), and one coworker.

10. For more see Carmina Salcido and Steve Jackson, *Not Lost Forever: My Story of Survival* (New York: HarperCollins, 2009).

11. The word *theodicy* refers to any formal attempt to explain why God allows evil.

12. *The God Delusion* (Boston: Mariner, 2008), 89.

Let's reflect more on the problem of evil and the attempted murder of young Carmina. Imagine having your throat slit by your own father and being left for dead beside your two murdered siblings. Psalm 139:16 takes on a completely different tone when we contemplate it in light of Carmina's life. Standard views of providence oblige us to say that our heavenly Father wrote in his book the intimate details of every day of Carmina's life, including April 15, 1989. In other words, on the day Carmina's throat was slit we can say, "The LORD has done what he planned…, which he decreed long ago." Nothing escapes God's perfect knowledge and power, and it all fits into his plan to manifest his own glory. From eternity God had planned that Ramon would take Carmina and her siblings out to that field. Even as she was knit together in her mother's womb, God had decreed that the knife would slice through her neck. And an eternity before she celebrated her first birthday, he foresaw every detail of the thirty-six hours that this innocent three-year-old would lie motionless in the dirt beside her two dead sisters.

Understandably, Christians often respond to such horrible evils by looking for the silver lining in the dark clouds or seeing the cup as half-full rather than half-empty. Yes, it is true that Carmina's two sisters were killed, but *she* managed to survive. And even if she was horribly scarred both physically and emotionally, does this survival not itself count as a miracle in the midst of tragedy? In that way Christians are able to turn the most heinous tragedies into arguments *for* God's providential care. Nor are Christians the only ones who do this. Consider how the media have the tendency to dub any good news in a horrendous tragedy as a "miracle." For instance, in June 2009 a Yemenia Airways Airbus A310 crashed into the ocean, killing 152 passengers and crew. However, there was one survivor, a thirteen-year-old girl, who was quickly dubbed a miracle by the media (though having been injured and lost her mother, she probably didn't find her own survival particularly miraculous).[13] It is understandable that a God-skeptic would find this to be a rather blatant example of the theist's confirmation bias in which any good news in a tragedy is a miraculous silver lining, no matter how big and dark the cloud it comes with. This sets Christians up for the following satirical argument for God's existence:

> *Argument from Incomplete Devastation:* A plane crashed killing 143 passengers and crew. But one child survived with only third-degree burns. Therefore God exists.[14]

This obviously absurd argument is intended to prompt an important question: Why does the bare survival of one child count *for* God while the brutal death of 143 (or 152) people does not count *against* God? The lesson is not that Christians need to rethink the standard view of providence—that's not my point. Even if the origin of evil remains shrouded in mystery, we can retain our hope and conviction that God is indeed working all things for his sovereign purposes. And I would say this: whatever anyone concludes about evil and its place in God's providential universe, let us Christians never pretend that we have *all* the answers, still less that we have *easy* answers.

Coda

In one memorable *Peanuts* cartoon, Charlie Brown walks up to Snoopy as the dog sits on his doghouse and plucks away at a typewriter. Charlie then says that he heard Snoopy is writing a book on theology and that he hopes the dog has chosen a good title. In response Snoopy types: "Has it ever occurred to you that you might be wrong?" This is a great question, and every Christian who is serious about the truth needs to

---

13. See "'Miracle' Plane Crash Survivor Back in France," http://www.cnn.com/2009/WORLD/europe/07/02/yemen.plane.survivor/index.html.

14. The argument, which is drawn from an atheist website, is cited by Dawkins, *The God Delusion*, 109.

ask it of him- or herself. Not surprisingly, atheists have been quick to make the point. Daniel Dennett commented: "History gives us many examples of large crowds of deluded people egging one another on down the primrose path to perdition. How can you be so sure you're not part of such a group? I for one am not in awe of your faith. I am appalled by your arrogance, by your unreasonable certainty that you have all the answers."[15] Setting aside the overly polemical tone of Dennett's comments, he certainly makes a legitimate point. As I have argued, it is a point that a Christian should be well prepared to contemplate. But, by the same token, I wonder if Dennett has considered that the point could be applied equally to him. Has he considered whether *he* as an atheist might be part of a large group of deluded people? Or are atheists never deluded? Have atheists no bias? Of course they do. If we want to take our own confirmation bias seriously, we need to get over our penchant for finding it in another and take a closer look at ourselves. Otherwise we—Christian, atheist, or anybody else—will end up looking as ridiculous as the man who remains oblivious to the block of wood protruding from his head, even as he scans passersby for the tiniest fleck of sawdust on an eyelash.

---

15. Dennett, *Breaking the Spell: Religion as a Natural Phenomenon* (New York: Penguin, 2006), 51.

4

NOT EVERYTHING IS **BLACK AND WHITE**

It was a Sunday much like any other. I was a university student pulling in late (as usual, I must admit) to the large suburban church I attended. As I cruised slowly around the packed parking lot, looking for a space, I quickly began to grow more frustrated with the passing of each occupied stall. Then I saw it, a spot that somehow everybody else had missed. Immediately my car lurched forward like a hawk closing in on its prey. Then just as quickly I had to slam on the brakes as I realized that my "empty" spot was actually occupied—at least partially. To my utter dismay and considerable anger, a shiny red Corvette was parked diagonally in this packed church parking lot, *taking up two spaces.* Perhaps, I might understand such behavior on a Monday afternoon at the shopping mall, but on a *Sunday morning at church?*

So there I sat in my idling automobile, outraged by this incredibly obnoxious and egotistical act. But even if I was forced to surrender my claim on the parking spot, I was not going to retreat until I had at least secured the moral high ground. And so after I angrily parked my car in the empty lot across the street (a good *five-minute walk* from the church, mind you), I penned a note of brotherly admonition that I tucked under the fancy windshield wiper of this egregious offender's sports car. The note went something like this:

My dearest brother in Christ,

I offer you this admonition in the spirit of Christian love and grace. While I recognize that you might deem it necessary to park your fine automobile in two spots on most days, I would implore you to take up one spot on Sundays in the spirit of Christian love.

With all blessings,

Your anonymous brother in Christ

Okay, maybe my memory has softened the tone of the note somewhat. But even if it was a wee bit more confrontational, it was surely justified. After all, I was merely presenting the spirit of pure, righteous indignation exemplified by the biblical prophets. Whoever this fellow was—whether he be a musclebound meathead or a fifty-year-old banker living his second childhood—he needed a little instruction in the school of Christ, and I was happy to provide it. And so, with my duty done (complemented by a healthy dose of moral superiority), I left the note on the windshield and entered the church to join in choruses of praise to the Lord.

At that point I quickly forgot about the whole affair . . . until the service the following week. After the morning music the pastor took the microphone and began to tell us about an elderly woman in the congregation who had broken her hip a few weeks before. When her car broke down, the woman borrowed her son's Corvette to get to church. (Suddenly I began to pay very close attention.) Alas, with her bad hip the only way to get the car door open was by swinging it all the way out. But since Corvette doors are notoriously long and heavy, she was reasonably worried that a door swung fully open would hit the car parked beside her. (At this point I began slouching low in the pew while trying my best to appear casual.) And so, she came to church early and parked on the far edge of the parking lot, taking up two spots so she could swing the door open after church without hitting another car. And even after all her efforts at doing the right thing, she still received a self-righteous, handwritten reprimand from an anonymous congregant.

Oops.

Now in my defense it must be said: *Who on earth, upon seeing a Corvette taking up two spots, would ever suspect that it was being driven by a little old lady with a broken hip?* But perhaps that was just the point: reality is very often more complex than we first suppose. And when you realize that a Corvette taking up two spots just might be driven by an elderly woman, you are forced to rethink many other overly simplified judgments about the world.

I have often reminded myself of this incident whenever I have been tempted to judge a situation prematurely with those stark categories of true or false, good or bad, right or wrong. My encounter with that Corvette provided a vivid reminder that very often a situation or issue is more complex than that, and so I need to resist jumping to conclusions prior to seeking all the evidence. And perhaps that means that I should not judge the driver of a Corvette (even when the car is taking up two spots at church) until I know something of the person and his or her circumstances. But the lesson extends far beyond the parking lot. This tendency that allows us to marginalize the unseen drivers of obnoxiously parked cars also allows us to marginalize individuals for holding particular philosophical, political, or religious opinions. So we move seamlessly from "Only a self-absorbed jerk would park like that" to "Only a moron would vote for that political candidate" or "No morally serious person could ever worship at that church." Stark, unqualified statements like these tend to signal the presence of inexcusably simple binary opposites. (Of course, there are cases where the choice is stark, but they are exceptions.) These judgments are, in short, the next step in the manifestation of the unchecked confirmation bias. And if they are not dealt with critically, they will inhibit our ability to hear and learn from others. So the person concerned to develop a truthful character must chasten these sweeping judgments, and that shall be our focus in this chapter. Unchecked confirmation biases and binary oppositions leave us terribly vulnerable to indoctrination. We will consider three key elements in the origin of indoctrination. Next, we will illustrate the widespread and multifarious nature of indoctrination by considering indoctrinational elements in contemporary atheism and evangelicalism. Finally, I will explain how indoctrination is especially inimical to the truth-seeking spirit of Christianity.

Are You Brainwashed?

Greta had lived all her life on her family's bucolic Iowa farm. While in her years growing up she had found serenity in the rustle of the corn-fields and the endless blue sky, as she entered her teen years restlessness began to grow within her. By the time she entered her senior year in high school, she longed to leave the rural life and travel out west to California. And so the day after graduation she boarded a bus with one modest duffle bag and high hopes. When she arrived in Santa Monica three days later, she was dazzled by the California sun and palm trees, and for the first few weeks she spent most afternoons at the beach. Then one day while walking in the surf, Greta met a kind and charismatic bearded man named Zotar, who quickly swept her off her feet with his sharp wit, piercing blue eyes (were those color contacts?), and expansive knowledge of Eastern philosophy. It didn't take long for Greta to agree to attend a small-group study with Zotar and his friends. From that point on things happened fast: within a week Greta (now christened "Rainbow") had moved into Zotar's commune and cut off all contact with her family and friends. Zotar explained that this separation was necessary because the world was full of "darks"— that is, those not yet enlightened by Zotar's truth. Since only Zotar and his disciples were the "enlightened ones," it was their obligation to bring salvation to the world. Consequently, they could not risk being corrupted by unmonitored interaction with the darks, even when those darks were an individual's immediate family. But Zotar assured

Rainbow that once her enlightenment was complete, she would be free to share the true light with her bewildered family.

Those who hear Greta's story will likely conclude that she has been brainwashed. While this term carries with it all sorts of negative connotations, a more precise (if less dramatic) diagnosis is that Greta has been indoctrinated. While terms like *brainwashed* and *indoctrinated* prompt images of glazed-eyed, naive disciples sitting at the feet of a pretentious prophet, in reality indoctrination is a much more common and subtle phenomenon than most people realize. In my estimation, it evinces three common characteristics. It begins with an inability to think critically about certain core ideological beliefs because these beliefs are deemed off limits from critical introspective analysis. As a result, while indoctrinated people may be brilliant critical thinkers in a variety of areas, they are nonetheless unable to think critically about certain aspects of their key beliefs. Second, these core beliefs are typically protected from critical introspection by way of an absolute binary opposition between truth and error, right and wrong, good and evil. Finally, resistance to these binary opposites that protect the core ideological beliefs is typically lowered if we sense an imminent crisis that demands quick action. The idea is that since times of imminent threat do not allow us the luxury of nuance, we should accept the binary absolutes as rough-and-ready, necessary approximations, at least until the crisis has passed. Unfortunately, this is a Catch-22, for once we accept such distorting categories, they are very difficult to renounce or transcend. Such is the Faustian pact of indoctrination.

At this point we'll consider each of these characteristics in more depth, beginning with the key element of inhibiting our critical thinking faculties from critically examining our beliefs. As Elmer Thiessen observed, "Indoctrination . . . is thought to involve the failure to produce minds that are open and critical."[16] As I suggested,

---

16. Thiessen, *In Defense of Religious Schools and Colleges* (Montreal and Kingston: McGill-Queen's University Press, 2001), 134.

this point needs qualification since indoctrination typically leaves critical thinking skills uninhibited in many areas. For instance, Zotar could count among his faithful disciples a well-respected lawyer and a brilliant mathematician, both of whom are the very embodiment of logicality—*except* when it concerns allegiance to their prophet. While education is truth directed and concerned with teaching people how to think, indoctrination is ideology directed and primarily focused on teaching them what to think. Thus to the extent that a curriculum or pedagogue inhibits our ability to think critically about the core assumptions of the system or ideology, it is to that degree indoctrinational.

Greta's new beliefs about Zotar's messiahship provide a vivid example of this first step of indoctrination. Rather than encourage Greta to evaluate his teaching carefully and critically, Zotar has stressed that his beliefs are infallible and that his authority is absolute; therefore, he is not to be questioned. The last thing Zotar wants is for Greta to think rationally and objectively by seeking external, corroborative evidence to back up his extraordinary claims. As a result, Greta is simply unable to subject her beliefs about Zotar to critical scrutiny. Because of Zotar's conditioning, she is unable to consider her family's impassioned and reasoned appeals. "This guy is messing with your head, Greta!" (Zotar warned her they would say that.) "He's a leader of a dangerous little cult." (Of course, they'd say *that*. Zotar said they are still in the darkness.) "Greta, we love you!" (Lies, all lies. Only Zotar loves Greta. *He told her so.*)

This brings us to the second point. The single most effective way to protect a core set of ideological claims from critical introspection is by positing a simplistic binary opposition between two sides while placing the views we seek to protect on the correct or true side and all views hostile to the core ideology on the incorrect or false side. Common and highly effective binary opposites include truth/lies, good/evil, intelligent/stupid, and light/darkness. That is, in the binary opposition one position is counted true, good, intelligent, and light, while the other is (or *all others are*) considered to be a lie, evil, stupid, and/or dark. Once these binary categories are in place—with the inviolable core ideological claims safely ensconced on the side of truth, goodness, intelligence, and light—all the dissent from the other side can be speedily dismissed. So once Greta has accepted Zotar's fundamental division of the world into the "lights" and the "darks," she has critically inhibited herself from questioning her own indoctrination. At this point the most reasoned entreaties can be dismissed as nothing more than seductive assaults from the forces of darkness.

Of course, there are real instances where we really must choose between two stark options, one of which is clearly right and the other clearly wrong. The problem arises when an absolute binary opposition extends such divisions to an untenable degree while critically distorting the nuances that so often attend real life. (To recall our opening example, I learned the hard way that not every Corvette that is parked to take up two spots is driven by a moron.) So, at the very core of the indoctrinational binary opposition is the division into the right/good position (that which is held by the indoctrinator and indoctrinated) and the wrong/evil position (that which is held by everybody else).

Clearly the binary opposition is critical to Greta's indoctrination. If Zotar had stressed that he could be wrong and that others could be right; if he had advised her to listen closely to the testimony her family and friends and weigh that testimony objectively against his; if he had encouraged her not to take his word for it but rather to seek external evidence that could corroborate his claims; and if he stressed that he could be right on some issues but wrong on others and it is Greta's duty to discern where the truth and error lies; if he had done all these things, then Greta would not have been indoctrinated. But clearly the last thing that Zotar wants is a freethinking disciple. So he protects his ideology by positing a stark binary distinction between the enlightened few who completely accept his views and the darkened world that rejects them.

Once people accept a binary opposition, they are rendered unable to challenge the core ideology that it protects. But that begs the question of how rational, educated people are ever persuaded to accept a binary opposition to begin with. Surely they can see the trick coming from a mile away, can't they? Can't they see how obviously untenable it is? While this is typically true, the rigor of analytic criticism appears to drop precipitously the moment people sense a perceived crisis. When people feel under threat, they are much more likely to find ways to restore stability and order, and this makes them much more liable to accept the security offered by a simplistic binary opposition. The reasoning is simple: in the time of crisis we simply do not have the luxury to recognize every little qualification or nuance. For the time being we need a firm place on which to stand so that we may distinguish the "good guys" from the "bad guys." Once we get our bearings and the danger has passed, then we can again afford the luxury of qualifying or nuancing our categories.

By creating this heightened sense of urgency, people are subtly coerced or cajoled into accepting the proposed binary categorization. A state of war provides the archetypal example. In the wake of the terrible events of 9/11, George W. Bush made his famous declaration at a joint session of the Congress on September 20, 2001: "Either you are with us, or you are with the terrorists."[17] With this statement Bush implied that anybody who disagreed with his government's policies was *de facto* sympathizing with the 9/11 terrorists: there simply was no middle ground. Once people had accepted this either/or opposition, as many (including representatives from the mainstream media) did, it was easy enough to silence opposition. (Who wants to be seen on the side of terrorists?) This sadly led to a quashing of much-needed public debate over the best diplomatic and military response (in Afghanistan and Iraq in particular), in the name of patriotism. As

---

17. The famous clip is available on YouTube at http://www.youtube.com/watch?v=cpPABLW6F_A.

Barbara Ehrenreich put it: "I trace the outbreak of droidlike confor-
mity to the aftermath of 9/11, when groupthink became the official
substitute for patriotism and we began to run out of surfaces for af-
fixing American flags."[18] To take one memorable example from this
heady period, the very popular country music group Dixie Chicks
faced record burnings, a radio blackout, and even death threats after
lead singer Natalie Maines dared to denounce George Bush publicly
at a 2003 concert.[19] In retrospect, it should have been obvious that
criticism of the government or commander in chief did not necessarily imply a lack of patriotism, let alone support for the terrorists. But,
at the time, in the midst of the crisis and fear, this point did not seem
obvious at all. Only as the initial sense of crisis has dissipated have
more people come to regret deeply the initial complicity with this
stark binary opposition.

One of the concerns with the so-called war on terror is that there
is no clearly defined enemy or goal in fighting. Without a definite goal
this war sets the stage for a *perpetual* state of crisis and with it an ongoing vulnerability to absolute binary opposites and the indemnification
of ideological claims from critical scrutiny. As Roderick Hindery
observed, a state of perpetual crisis breeds a "conspiratorial them-
against-us mentality"[20] that often leads to "a simplistic, Manichean
division of people into two classes."[21] When it comes to conservative
Christianity, the notion of a culture war with clearly defined sides
(e.g., the church versus the world) that are in a perpetual crisis renders

---

18. *This Land Is Their Land: Reports from a Divided Nation* (New York: Metropolitan
Books, 2008), 214.

19. See the 2006 documentary *Shut Up & Sing*.

20. Roderick Hindery, "The Anatomy of Propaganda within Religious Terrorism," *The
Humanist* (March/April 2003): 17.

21. Hindery, "The Anatomy of Propaganda within Religious Terrorism," 17.

Christians vulnerable to equally bald categories of indoctrination.[22] Such divisions simply have a devastating impact on critical thinking.

When Zotar introduced Greta to his philosophy, he could have done so with a mild "come and join us" invitation. But this clearly lacks the essential sense of urgency necessary to maximize receptivity. If there is no pressing crisis pushing Greta on to join Zotar this minute, she will be less likely to accept the simple dichotomies he offers that protect his core ideological assertions about his own messiahship. Zotar knew that she was already vulnerable as a naive stranger from the Midwest, far from her support network, and so he immediately began to exploit that vulnerability. To go that next step and posit a crisis situation between the darks and lights adds the sense of urgency that makes Greta more likely to accept indoctrination. So Zotar warns of a coming crisis, limited time, polarized choices, and an impending battle, all of which serve to draw Greta uncritically into his ideology.

One final note: the exploitation of crisis is not limited to cult leaders and governments. Indeed, it is used every day in retail sales. Take the car salesperson who pressures a potential customer by telling her that somebody else just put in an offer on the car that piqued her interest. This may not be true, but it serves to initiate a modest crisis situation for the bedazzled consumer who cannot bear losing that shiny convertible and may, as a result, be pressured into making a hasty purchase. (Consequently, consumer advocates fight in various jurisdictions for "cooling-off periods" during which a consumer is able to back out of a contract he or she was drawn into through coercive crisis techniques.) While such manipulation of the consumer is serious, it is a whole different order of significance when that which is being sold is not a product but a set of beliefs—an ideology—that will

---

22. Chris Hedges provides a number of examples where evangelicals appropriate binary militaristic language that furthers the sense of crisis and culture war in *American Fascists: The Christian Right and the War on America* (New York: Free Press, 2008), 29–30.

delimit and inhibit people's critical thinking in perpetuity. Tragically, Zotar offered Greta no cooling-off period.

Indoctrinated Atheists

Buying into a California beach cult lock, stock, and barrel may be an uncontroversial case of indoctrination, but our own epistemic (or belief) communities have their own vulnerabilities. The problem with indoctrination (like the confirmation bias) is that it is one of those things we see much more readily in others than in ourselves. Nobody wants to admit indoctrination in his or her own epistemic community, and, to the extent that we ourselves are affected by it, we may be unable to see it. But the type of careful examination that is necessary for self-diagnosis is critical. In this section I am going to take a look at indoctrination in the contemporary resurgence of atheism known as "the new atheism."[23] It is true that atheism is not a unified ideology, let alone an institution. But that does not mean it is not liable to indoctrination; indeed, the lack of formal institution, creed, or leader may cultivate a false sense of autonomy that renders a person *more* liable to indoctrination. What is necessary for indoctrination is not a magisterium or sacred text but simply a set of teachings that inhibits critical thought, and I will argue that the new atheism clearly exudes this ignominious characteristic.

One of the most effective ways to inure an ideology from critical appraisal is by convincing those who hold it that it is not a set of beliefs in need of defense but rather a common-sense conclusion. (Surely common sense needs no defense.) And so it is not surprising that a number of new atheists stress that atheism is nothing more than good sense. This is how Sam Harris put it:

---

23. The new atheism is a strident, antireligious form of atheism that has emerged as a force in popular culture since 9/11 and that is represented by its four leaders, Richard Dawkins, Daniel Dennett, Sam Harris, and Christopher Hitchens.

> Atheism is not a philosophy; it is not even a view of the world; it is simply an admission of the obvious. In fact, "atheism" is a term that should not even exist. No one ever needs to identify himself as a "non-astrologer" or a "non-alchemist." We do not have words for people who doubt that Elvis is still alive or that aliens have traversed the galaxy only to molest ranchers and their cattle. Atheism is nothing more than the noises reasonable people make in the presence of unjustified religious beliefs.[24]

If atheism is simply "an admission of the obvious," it needs no defense, and those who deny it are *de facto* standing in direct opposition to the obvious. Along the same lines, David Mills argued that "atheists have no obligation to prove or disprove anything. Otherwise—if you demand belief in all Beings for which there is no absolute *dis*-proof—then you are forced by your own twisted 'logic' to believe in mile-long pink elephants on Pluto, since, at present, we haven't explored Pluto and shown them to be nonexistent."[25] Like Harris, Mills aimed to demonstrate that the atheist is not obliged to defend anything. In their view, atheism is simply common sense, while theistic belief is absurd.

These convictions concerning the radically different epistemic status of disbelief and belief indemnify core atheistic assumptions from serious scrutiny by functioning as an effective binary opposite: in short, atheism is common sense, while every system of thought short of atheism is irrational or unjustified. And so, we have the pivotal binary opposition between the rational atheist and the irrational theist (or, as Richard Dawkins has described the latter, the "faith head"). In this new atheist view the religious individual is bound by the cognitive

---

24. Harris, *Letter to a Christian Nation* (New York: Alfred A. Knopf, 2006), 51.
25. David Mills, *Atheist Universe: The Thinking Person's Answer to Christian Fundamentalism* (Berkeley: Ulysses, 2006), 29.

chains of irrational dogma, while the atheist skeptic is unencumbered by any dogmas and thus is free to countenance the evidence without bias. The view is memorably stated by Barbara Ehrenreich in a reflection on her own irreligious upbringing:

> I was raised in a real strong Secular Humanist family—the kind of folks who'd ground you for a week just for thinking of dating a Unitarian, or worse. Not that they were hard-liners, though. We had over 70 Bibles lying around the house where anyone could browse through them—Gideons my dad had removed from the motel rooms he'd stayed in. And I remember how he gloried in every Gideon he lifted, thinking of all the traveling salesmen whose minds he'd probably saved from dry rot.
>
> Looking back, I guess you could say I never really had a choice, what with my parents always preaching, "Think for yourself! Think for yourself!"[26]

Ehrenreich's "think for yourself" mantra provides a clear example of the atheist's myth of freethinking autonomy that makes them especially vulnerable to indoctrination. As such, it provides an excellent introduction to the first step in indoctrination, atheist-style. On the surface "think for yourself" would sound like an excellent inoculation against indoctrination, for it seems to commend the exercise of an individual's own critical thinking rather than bowing to the blind acceptance of authority. But even as Ehrenreich proclaimed her cognitive autonomy, she implicitly acknowledged that her parents were as dogmatic as any, snatching Bibles from hotel rooms and proscribing social interaction with those of religious faith. Ironically, the mantra "think for yourself" can be a very effective tool of indoctrination

---

26. Barbara Ehrenreich, "Give Me That New-Time Religion," *Mother Jones* (June/July 1987): 60.

insofar as it masks the inevitable formation by a person's upbringing, mentors, and life experience.

Consequently, new atheists could hardly be more withering in their assessment of religious conviction. The depth of the binary opposition is captured in the following Robert Pirsig statement that Richard Dawkins quoted with approval: "When one person suffers from a delusion, it is called insanity. When many people suffer from a delusion it is called Religion."[27] Similarly Sam Harris described "the history of Christian theology" as "the story of bookish men parsing a collective delusion."[28] And if the notion of religion as a collective delusion were not bad enough, Dawkins also claimed that religion is like a mind virus that co-opts and corrupts the mind of its host like a parasite.[29] While the atheist is supposed to be the liberated freethinker, the religious believer is enslaved to a mass, collective delusion that borders on *insanity*.

Not surprisingly, given that the religiously devout suffer from a cognitive delusion, their expostulations on matters metaphysical are to be taken with no greater seriousness than the mental patient mumbling in the corner of the sanatorium. With this assumption atheists can dismiss with staggering glibness the entire discipline of theology. For instance, Dawkins referred to the ontological argument for God's existence, an argument that has fascinated many of the most astute philosophical minds for the last eight hundred years, merely as "infantile."[30] Moreover, he claimed that "the notion that religion is a proper *field* in which one might claim *expertise*, is one that should not go unquestioned. That clergyman presumably would not have deferred to the expertise of a claimed 'fairyologist' on the exact shape

---

27. Cited in Dawkins, *The God Delusion* (Boston: Mariner, 2008), 28.
28. Harris, *Letter to a Christian Nation*, 5.
29. See "Viruses of the Mind," in *A Devil's Chaplain: Reflections on Hope, Lies, Science, and Love* (New York: Houghton Mifflin, 2003), 128–151.
30. Dawkins, *The God Delusion*, 104.

and color of fairy wings."[31] Obviously it is a waste of time to get into a serious debate with somebody who insists on the existence of fairies (even if he or she happens to claim expertise in those matters). In the paperback version of *The God Delusion*, Dawkins responded directly to the charge that he had been inappropriately dismissive of theology by writing: "I would happily have forgone bestsellerdom if there had been the slightest hope of Duns Scotus illuminating my central question of whether God exists."[32] So, according to Dawkins there is literally no hope that so eminent a theologian as Duns Scotus (the famed "subtle doctor" of the thirteenth century) could have *anything* enlightening to say on the question of God's existence.

The categories are ideologically effective for those who accept them, for they allow even the most novice atheist to dismiss the most senior theologians as deluded fools and irrational know-nothings. So we have David Mills, commenting: "Nor, in my opinion, is it even possible to change the religious views of those who perceive themselves as ethically superior because they belong to the one 'true' religion. Their ears and eyes and minds are closed forever. No amount of science or logic will make any difference to them."[33] Note how Mills categorically dismissed anybody who assents to a formal religious faith as hopelessly beyond the reach of rational argument. Other examples of this strategy of marginalization are easy to find. In *God Is Not Great*, Christopher Hitchens asserted, "Religion comes from the period of human prehistory where nobody . . . had the smallest idea what was going on."[34] This sweeping statement allowed Hitchens to conclude that "all attempts to reconcile faith with science and reason

---

31. Dawkins, *The God Delusion*, 37.
32. Dawkins, *The God Delusion,* 14.
33. Mills, *Atheist Universe*, 21.
34. Hitchens, *God Is Not Great: How Religion Poisons Everything* (New York: Twelve, 2007), 64.

are consigned to failure and ridicule."[35] So the same binary opposition that enabled Dawkins to dismiss theologians as idiots allowed Hitchens to ignore anybody (scientists included) who would seek to reconcile science with religion. You might as well attempt to reconcile science with alchemy.[36]

We certainly find ample evidence for the first two dimensions of indoctrination in the new atheists given their "irrational faith versus reasonable common sense" dichotomy. But do we find evidence for the crisis situation that makes people more receptive to these binary categories to begin with? Indeed, a sense of crisis is significant for the new atheism. It is important to understand that the new atheism is a post-9/11 phenomenon spurred on by the fear that the unchecked growth of religious fundamentalism will lead to increasing violence. Consequently, the new atheism reflects a new level of stridency against religion, driven by the fear of religious violence and oppression. Dawkins thus explained his animus toward religion: "[S]uch hostility as I or other atheists occasionally voice towards religion is limited to words. I am not going to bomb anybody, behead them, stone them, burn them at the stake, crucify them, or fly planes into their skyscrapers, just because of a theological disagreement."[37]

Critics of religion like Dawkins appeal to this fear of imminent violence arising from the teeming hordes of the religiously devout as the reason for forgoing nuance and charity. (You don't mind your p's and q's when you're in a life-or-death struggle with the glazed-eyed religious zealot.) At the beginning of his book *Breaking the Spell* (the spell being religion), philosopher Daniel Dennett provided a revealing admission: "Perhaps I should have devoted several more years to study

---

35. Hitchens, *God Is Not Great*, 64–5.

36. Not to be outdone, Sam Harris claims that "the central tenet of every religious tradition is that all others are mere repositories of error or, at best, dangerously incomplete. Intolerance is thus intrinsic to every creed." *The End of Faith: Religion, Terror, and the Future of Reason* (New York: Norton, 2006), 13.

37. Dawkins, *The God Delusion*, 318.

[of religion] before writing this book, but *since the urgency of the message was borne in on me again and again by current events*, I had to settle for the perspectives I had managed to achieve so far."[38] So presumably Dennett's often blunt, dichotomistic treatment of religion should be excused because he did not have the luxury of more in-depth study, given the state of crisis posed by fundamentalism.

The predictable result of new atheist indoctrination is an inability to take the views of the religiously devout seriously. We find ample evidence of this in Dawkins's book *The God Delusion*. For instance, Dawkins described his puzzlement with religiously devout scientists as follows: "I remain *baffled*, not so much by their belief in a cosmic lawgiver of some kind, as by their belief in the details of the Christian religion: resurrection, forgiveness of sins and all."[39] Nor can Dawkins understand those theists who believe God could have used evolution to create: "I am continually *astonished* by those theists who, far from having their consciousness raised in the way that I propose, seem to rejoice in natural selection as 'God's way of achieving his creation.'"[40] Dawkins was even mystified that some Christians could actually be highly educated: "Why any circles worthy of the name of sophisticated remain within the Church is a *mystery* at least as deep as those that theologians enjoy."[41] Dawkins's mystification carried over to the high levels of religious observance within the American population: "The religiosity of today's America is something truly *remarkable*."[42] Note the terms I italicized in these quotes: *baffled, astonished, mystery, remarkable*. In these less-than-subtle ways Dawkins marginalized the religiously devout as a bizarre phenomenon that resists rational ex-

---

38. Dennett, *Breaking the Spell: Religion as a Natural Phenomenon* (New York: Penguin, 2006), xiv, emphasis added.

39. Dawkins, *The God Delusion*, 125, emphasis added.

40. Dawkins, *The God Delusion*, 143–144, emphasis added. We will look at this question of Darwinian Christians in chapter 8.

41. Dawkins, *The God Delusion*, 84, emphasis added.

42. Dawkins, *The God Delusion*, 26, emphasis added.

planation, rather like the dual nature of light as wave and particle. So indoctrinated was he, so unable to consider a person holding a theistic view as being rational let alone intelligent, that he was constrained by the perplexity of his own crude categories.

Indoctrinated Evangelicals

It is surely ironic that new atheists like Richard Dawkins, who pride themselves on being great defenders of truth and reason, actually reveal the classic hallmarks of indoctrination. But before we relish this irony too much, we should note that these same marks can be found in the evangelical neck of the woods. For this example closer to home we'll consider Focus on the Family's *The Truth Project*. I will focus my discussion on session one of the curriculum, which is devoted to the lofty topic of veritology (or truth). Against this backdrop I will argue that the curriculum reveals the three marks of indoctrination as it insulates core ideological commitments from further critical intro-spection by way of a tendentious binary opposition that is spurred on by a perpetual crisis of good versus evil.

The core ideological commitment of *The Truth Project* is found in the notion that, while the world is fallen in lies and darkness, Christ came to establish the church as a beachhead of his beacon of truth. The starkness with which this vision is developed leads naturally to a binary opposition between truth and error, which Del Tackett drew primarily from the Johannine writings. For instance, in John 18:37 Jesus declared: "The reason I was born and came into the world is to testify to the truth. Everyone on the side of truth listens to me." According to Tackett, when Jesus made this statement, he bifurcated the world into two diametrically opposed sides that Tackett defined as "Truth/Reality" and "Lies/Illusion." Consider how starkly Tackett divided these two groups:

> This is a battle of worldviews. It is a battle between the
> truth claims of God and the lies and the illusions of the

world of flesh and the devil. On this side the truth claims of God are consistent and logical. They make sense. They work. And even in a fallen world when we follow them they lead to peace and prosperity and happiness. And opposed to that, the web of lies of the world of flesh and the devil. And it is illogical, it has holes in it, it is inconsistent and it leads to the most grievous weeping, wailing and moaning and death. (session one)

It is intriguing to consider how much Tackett's words sound like an excerpt from a speech we might expect Zotar to deliver to his devotees. For one thing, Tackett allowed only two sides: the side of truth and God and the side of lies and the Devil. We might want to interject immediately, "But aren't there many different worldviews, and aren't some of them *more* correct than others? For instance, surely a Jew is closer to the truth than an atheist." This comprehensive categorization of all dissent from the Christian view as the lies of the Devil is disturbing when it comes from Zotar; but is it any less disturbing when it comes from Tackett as he instructs thousands upon thousands of evangelical Christians in the name of a mature and nuanced Christian worldview?

Let's look further at the neat and absolute way that Tackett's binary opposition divides opinions: "On this side the truth claims of God are consistent and logical. They make sense. They work. And even in a fallen world when we follow them they lead to peace and prosperity and happiness." Taken literally this statement is demonstrably false since not every faithful Christian experiences peace, prosperity, and happiness: many instead undergo terrible, agonizing lives. The painful reality is that many will not achieve peace, prosperity, and happiness on this side of eternity as Revelation 21:4 suggests. In fact, the notion of imminent guaranteed blessing also sounds like something we would expect to hear from a charlatan preacher or a cultic leader like Zotar: "Follow me, my children, and peace, prosperity, and happiness are all yours. But turn away from me and to the world of devils and darkness, and you will face grievous weeping, wailing and moaning and death."

To put it bluntly, Del Tackett's absolute dichotomizing of the world into polar opposites could be effectively utilized by a cult leader seeking to control the faithful. This is not to suggest that *The Truth Project* is sociologically cultic, though its pedagogical characteristics are undeniably indoctrinational. Think again about the effectiveness by which Dawkins marginalized every Christian as no different from a "fairyologist." While this is frustrating for the Christian, it is no worse than when Tackett stated that every atheist (and indeed everybody but the Christian) has no truth but rather is simply like a POW enslaved to the darkness. Not surprisingly, once this binary opposition is in place, Tackett's views are insulated from critical inquiry. What does it do to a person's thinking process to be instructed to think that a vast range of issues from theology to economics to history (some of the topics that *The Truth Project* itself includes) can all be neatly divided into the one completely true "Christian" position and the other completely false "non-Christian" alternative?

Finally, we turn to our third and last point: the perceived crisis that spurs people on to accept the proposed binary opposition. In the spirit of the new atheists who warn of a fomenting battle with violent religious fundamentalists, Tackett spoke of an approaching "Cosmic Battle" between forces of light and darkness. Within this battle Christians are the people of the truth (1 John 4:6), while everyone in the world (presumably everybody who is not a Christian including atheists, Muslims, and Jews) is locked in the darkness, waiting liberation. Since the battle is absolute, enduring, and the stakes are so high (ultimately concerning the destiny of eternal souls), this worldview is ideally suited to indoctrinational manipulation.

Are Christians Especially Prone to Indoctrination?

Our brief analysis of *The Truth Project* prompts us to ask whether Christians are *especially* susceptible to indoctrination. Put another way, maybe the issue is not with *The Truth Project* but rather with Christianity. After all, Del Tackett was not *inventing* the sweeping distinctions between the kingdom of God and the kingdom of the world. Rather, they were drawn straight from Scripture. So is the tendency toward indoctrination actually a greater danger for Christian belief? On the contrary, I will argue in three points that, while Christian theology does draw an important distinction of two kingdoms, properly understood this distinction actually *decreases* the tendency toward indoctrination.

Let's begin with the basic question of ideology. It is commonly assumed by atheists and other critics of religious beliefs that Christianity is rooted in an indoctrinational authoritarianism that suppresses independent thought. Thus new atheist Daniel Dennett provided an excellent example of this idea when he quoted the warning of a Christian writer named de Rougemont to his Christian brothers and sisters:

> If anybody ever raises questions or objections about our religion that you cannot answer, that person is almost certainly Satan. In fact, the more reasonable the person is, the more eager to engage you in open-minded and congenial discussion, the more sure you can be that you're talking to Satan in disguise! Turn away! Do not listen! It's a trap![43]

Clearly Dennett was anxious to pour derision on any simplistic binary opposition between the people of truth and the people of lies. As he caustically put it, "If I were designing a phony religion, I'd

---

43. Cited in Dennett, *Breaking the Spell*, 207.

surely include a version of this little gem—but I'd have a hard time saying it with a straight face."[44] And it is difficult not to sympathize with Dennett here. Are Christians really fated to this kind of indoctrinational marginalization of the other?

I actually agree with Dennett that this is unfortunate advice. The key mistaken belief in de Rougemont's warning is that it views deception wholly as an external danger, while never countenancing the real possibility of deception or mistaken belief arising from within the safe walls of our own fortress. Once we challenge this assumption, we undermine the entire indoctrinational framework. But before we can consider this point further, an immediate stumbling block appears. Doesn't Scripture itself anticipate de Rougemont's warning by prohibiting the kind of critical thinking necessary to prevent indoctrination? For instance, consider the following passage from Galatians:

> But even if we or an angel from heaven should preach a gospel other than the one we preached to you, let that person be under God's curse! As we have already said, so now I say again: If anybody is preaching to you a gospel other than what you accepted, let that person be under God's curse! (Galatians 1:8–9)

So here is the problem. If we object to de Rougemont's words, then we must likewise object to Paul's words of this absolute warning pleading unthinking fidelity to a set of claims. How can we escape this indoctrinational dilemma?

By way of response, we can begin by noting that Paul did not elevate his *own* authority. Instead, he stressed that every putative teacher must submit to the gospel. We see the same point when he commended the Bereans for testing his words in light of the evidence of the Scriptures (Acts 17:11). Here and elsewhere Paul commended critical thinking in the strongest possible terms. "Fair enough," the

---

44. Dennett, *Breaking the Spell*, 207.

atheist might reply. "Paul didn't elevate *himself* as the absolute authority. In other words, he didn't make himself the equivalent of Zotar. But he certainly *did* elevate the absolute, inviolable, and unquestionable authority of Scripture, thereby making Scripture equivalent to Zotar and making Christians mindless drones like Zotar's disciples. So de Rougemont was doing nothing different from what Paul would commend, and both commands are indoctrinational to the core."

The core of my response is that it is not the submission to authority that is the problem but rather the question of which authority we submit to and how we submit to it. Dennett's argument depends on the assumption that whatever authority Paul ascribed to the gospel is arbitrary, ungrounded, and ultimately unjustified. That is, it is no different from granting absolute fidelity to a societal reject you meet at the beach who declares himself the one true prophet. If we are to refute this notion, we must see how an unqualified assent to an authority can be a rational act. To see this, consider the following analogy. You have been tentatively accepted into an elite mountain-climbing apprenticeship with world-famous mountain climber Paul Peaks. But Mr. Peaks has one final condition prior to assenting to be your mentor: you must agree to accept all his instructions without question when you're up on the mountain. Given the ample evidence of Mr. Peaks's skill (including thirty years of successful climbs on the world's most difficult mountains), it would surely make good sense to assent to this request. I would contend that the authority the Christian grants the gospel is closer to the reasonable assent we would grant to Paul Peaks than the unreasonable assent we might grant to Zotar the prophet.

"If that claim is to be believed," replies the skeptic, "then what is this evidence for Jesus' authority that is analogous to the evidence of Paul Peaks's skill?" Great question. Let's begin with the observation that Jesus never demanded allegiance apart from evidence. He did not walk up to people and say, "I am Jesus, the Messiah. BELIEVE!" Rather, he established his authority through his exemplary character, his extraordinary teaching (Matthew 7:28; 13:54; 22:33; Mark 1:22; 11:18), the testimony of trusted authorities like John the Baptist (John 1:29), and the pivotal additional testimony of his sign miracles (see John 2:11; 3:2; 7:31; 9:16). To take one example, Jesus backed up his authority to forgive sins by performing a miraculous healing (Mark 2:10–12). And when doubters tried to explain away this evidence by claiming that Jesus was using the power of Satan, he rightly countered that such an explanation was incoherent, for it would entail that the Devil was working against his own interests (Luke 11:14–20). As important as all these miracles were for backing up the claims of Christ (and later of the apostles), the most important miracle was certainly Christ's resurrection from the dead: "After his suffering, he presented himself to them and gave many convincing proofs that he was alive" (Acts 1:3). These experiences of a resurrected Jesus sustained the apostles during much persecution, and it is these testimonies of Christ that Paul pointed to for evidence (1 Corinthians 15:5–7).[45] Scripture never commends the blind acceptance of authority.[46]

We could concede that Christianity is rooted in an initial appeal to evidence and still object that once you've bought into the system you are discouraged from further questioning regarding the truth of the gospel. But this too seems wrong. Paul clearly said, "If Christ has not been raised, our preaching is useless and so is your faith" (1 Corinthians 15:14). The implication of this statement is clear: if there

---

45. The church's beliefs in Christ are vindicated by rigorous historical inquiry. For an introductory assessment, see Lee Strobel, *The Case for Christ: A Journalist's Personal Investigation of the Evidence for Jesus* (Grand Rapids, MI: Zondervan, 1998).

46. Occasionally people extract the story of "doubting Thomas" from this wider evidential context to suggest that Christians belittle evidence: "Because you have seen me, you have believed; blessed are those who have not seen and yet have believed" (John 20:29). But even if those who are able to believe without evidence are blessed, that does not change the fact that evidence is provided for those seeking it. Moreover, we could argue that Thomas already had enough evidence to believe in the resurrection in light of the life and miracles of Jesus and the sober testimony of the other disciples to the resurrection. In that case, Jesus could be seen as willingly meeting even Thomas's excessive skepticism.

is serious evidence that Christ was not raised, Paul wants to know about it. If you have evidence that Paul Peaks is a huckster, you would want to know about it, for you recognize that your unconditional assent is dependent on his having a real history of mountain climbing and the skills that go with it. Thus Paul explained further in 1 Corinthians: "If Christ has not been raised, your faith is futile; you are still in your sins" (v. 17). He then argued that if Christians are wrong, we have testified falsely and "are to be pitied more than all others" (v. 18). Paul's assent to the gospel in Galatians 1 should be understood similarly. We place our trust in the gospel of Christ without qualification because of the evidence for its truth, but if contrary evidence were to arise, we would want to know about it. As a result, Paul's attitude could not contrast more starkly with that of the woman (in chapter three) who kiboshed the historical study of Jesus in an adult Sunday school class for fear of what she might discover.

There is a side to this commitment to the truth that some might find disconcerting. It is that openness to questioning and doubting of our own views. But perhaps we just have to reorient ourselves on this point by rejecting the assumption that doubt is the sign of an unhealthy faith. On the contrary, as Frederick Buechner observed, "Whether your faith is that there is a God or that there is not a God, if you don't have any doubts, you are either kidding yourself or asleep. Doubts are the ants in the pants of faith. They keep it awake and moving."[47] For an illustration, think of how an autonomous department of internal affairs is essential for a healthy police service. In much the same way, the eye of doubt and questioning is not an enemy to faith but a necessary component of its healthy functioning.

Now we can return to my initial observation that de Rougemont failed to recognize—that he could be wrong. It is certainly correct that Jesus introduced some striking dichotomies between truth/light/

47. Buechner, *Beyond Words: Daily Readings in the ABC's of Faith* (New York: HarperOne, 2004), 85. Thanks to Heather Seargeant for this reference.

God on the one hand, and lies/darkness/Devil on the other. So the problem lies not with the dichotomies per se, but rather with how we draw them. The point was memorably made by Harry Blamires:

> The Christian mind knows that, in any sorting out of the sheep and the goats, of the virtuous from the sinful, the forces of Heaven would slice through human society at an unexpected angle. The knife would cut firmly, but certainly not horizontally. What can we say or think of how it would separate the self-seekers from the fundamentally God-directed souls, except that it would certainly not leave all the convicts and perverts and public nuisances on one side, and all the cabinet ministers and business executives . . . on the other?[48]

And so while there most certainly is a legitimate binary opposition between the kingdom of God and the kingdom of the world, we cannot assume that because we are Christians we necessarily have a clear view of where that line is to be drawn. The point is absolutely essential because once we concede that we could be wrong (contrary to de Rougemont), we have a final hedge against indoctrination. The point is that we must all judge carefully for ourselves on an ongoing basis whether or not we are being faithful to the truth. If we must test the teachings of Jesus and Paul, then we certainly ought to test *all* contemporary authorities, including Zotar, Richard Dawkins, and Del Tackett, as well as our parents, pastors, teachers, and friends. And finally, we must test *ourselves*.

With that in mind, let's turn to the final concern that Christianity introduces a perpetual crisis between good and evil that makes people more vulnerable to the adoption of comfortably simple binary oppositions. Is this not a distinct problem for Christians? Doesn't it make them more susceptible to indoctrination? Isn't it clear that

---

48. Blamires, *The Christian Mind* (London: SPCK, 1963), 91.

Christianity commits us to a perpetual struggle between good and evil that will culminate in the great battle of Armageddon and with it worldwide cataclysmic destruction? And once we adopt that sense of an inevitable, impending crisis, are we not then rendered especially susceptible to indoctrination, given the urgency of our condition?

While Christian views on the end of the world differ, the essential point, by way of response, is that the consummation of all things depends not on us but on God's sovereign action. Time and again the message is that it is God's battle to win and that we are simply invited to participate in his victory. As God said through the psalmist, "Be still, and know that I am God; I will be exalted among the nations, I will be exalted in the earth" (Psalm 46:10). It is not up to us to be sure that God is exalted. He will surely take care of that. Likewise, Moses reminded the Israelites, "The LORD will fight for you; you need only to be still" (Exodus 14:14). And remember Mordecai's words to Esther when she was wrestling with whether to reveal Haman's murderous plot to King Xerxes: "For if you remain silent at this time, relief and deliverance for the Jews will arise from another place, but you and your father's family will perish. And who knows but that you have come to royal position for such a time as this?" (Esther 4:14). While thinking the victory depends on us might predispose us toward an indoctrinational pragmatism, this danger is removed when we realize that the burden of victory does not rest on our shoulders. As we trust the hands of divine sovereignty, we can be content with seeking to be faithful to the truth revealed in Christ.

Coda

It can seem a long way from a rash judgment on a Corvette's parking job to a glazed-eyed devotee of a cult leader. But it is very important that we see how the invocation of simplistic, black-and-white categories in mundane affairs can contribute to the invocation of similar categories in fundamental philosophical and religious perspectives.

While both atheists and evangelicals have often prided themselves (but not often the other) with being crusaders for intellectual objectivity, we have seen how both can be susceptible to indoctrination. Yes, there are absolute dichotomies to be drawn. There are a kingdom of light and a kingdom of darkness. There is truth and there is error. But does that mean that we always are in the light and always grasping truth? Hardly. There will come a day when we see face to face, and at that time we will be able to put concerns of indoctrination away. But for now we see darkly, and our judgments should always reflect this fact.

5

THOSE I DISAGREE WITH ARE **PROBABLY** NOT IGNORANT, IDIOTIC, INSANE, OR IMMORAL

Over the years Richard Dawkins has labored mightily to popularize the Darwinian theory of evolution and the atheistic worldview that he is convinced goes along with it. He has also become well known for his antagonism toward organized religion. Not surprisingly, he has never been one to soften his statements on religion for the sake of political correctness. This brings me to the following infamous statement that Dawkins made in a 1989 book review: "It is absolutely safe to say that if you meet somebody who claims not to believe in evolution, that person is ignorant, stupid or insane (or wicked, but I'd rather not consider that)."[1] This evocative statement provides a segue into the discussion of this chapter that considers how we often

---

1. Dawkins, review of *Blueprints: Solving the Mystery of Evolution* in *New York Times* (April 9, 1989), available online at http://www.memeoid.net/books/Dawkins/ Dawkins%20Articles/Review%20of%20Blueprints,%20Solving%20the%20 Mystery%20of%20Evolu.pdf.

marginalize those who disagree with us by assuming that they are either cognitively or morally incompetent.

Let's begin by thinking about Dawkins's statement a bit. If we were to take his stark options at face value, the claim would seem easy enough to falsify. All we need to do is identify one dissenter from Darwin who cannot plausibly be categorized as ignorant, idiotic, insane, or immoral. While I can think of many examples, I'll throw out just one for the sake of argument: young-earth creationist Paul Nelson. Nelson has a PhD from the University of Chicago, where he completed a dissertation in philosophy on macroevolutionary theory. Moreover, he is a popular speaker and debater on intelligent design theory. So if we limit ourselves to Dawkins's categories, where should we put Dr. Nelson? The first option is readily dispensed with: we cannot plausibly claim that Nelson is unfamiliar with the issues since he has a PhD in the area from a first-rate university. Nor are his impeccable credentials compatible with the claim that he is an idiot. As for insanity, how many people do you know who completed a PhD in science from one of the nation's leading universities while being clinically insane? With our other options exhausted, we are forced to contemplate the final possibility: Could it be that Paul Nelson is evil? While I do not know Dr. Nelson personally, I have watched him in interviews, and he certainly does not seem to me to be harboring malevolent intentions. This leaves me constrained to conclude that Dawkins's claim is simply false: Paul Nelson is an example of a dissenter from Darwin who is not ignorant, idiotic, insane, or immoral.

Once we get over the initial shock of Dawkins's statement, it is actually very helpful since it reflects a surprisingly common tendency that people have to dismiss dissent from their views by ascribing it to basic cognitive and/or moral incompetence. Before we cast the first stone at Dawkins, we should recognize that we are all tempted to dismiss those who persist in disagreeing with us on matters of deep conviction. It is easier to dismiss others either as cognitively deprived (perhaps ignorant, idiotic, or insane) or as plain immoral than it is to seek to understand them. For those interested in spotting bald cases of this type of marginalization, the highly polarized landscape of American politics presents a number of sobering examples. Indeed, the media bustles with popular pundits who issue sweeping pronouncements that consign dissenting voices to intellectual and/or moral oblivion. For instance, conservative pundit Ann Coulter's book *If Democrats Had Any Brains They'd Be Republicans*[2] implies that anybody who adopts a democratic perspective must do so out of incompetence (that is, out of *stupidity*). Not to be outdone, from the liberal camp Al Franken gives us *Lies and the Lying Liars Who Tell Them: A Fair and Balanced Look at the Right*,[3] a title that marginalizes many of those on the conservative right with the charge of immorality. Finally, not-so-honorable mention should go to Glenn Beck for his less-than-subtly titled contribution to ongoing political debate: *Arguing with Idiots.*[4]

Even if the general public often rewards a critical lack of nuance with high television ratings and book sales, we would hope that truth-seeking Christians would resist the temptation to chalk up a dissenter's opinion simply to ignorance, stupidity, psychosis, or evil. But, in point of fact, Christians often are, if anything, *more* likely to marginalize others with these kinds of sweeping judgments. Our concern in this chapter is to take a critical look at this tendency. This marginalization of the other comes as a natural outgrowth of the binary opposite that has already consigned the other as lost in error and lies. Once we accept this, we are constrained to explain dissent through these narrow categories. In this chapter we are going to attempt to move beyond this temptation to dismiss the views of the other as stupid or wicked. First, we will consider how those we deem idiots could be viewed as possibly intelligent (or at least not *completely* stupid). Next, we will

---

2. (New York: Crown, 2007).
3. (New York: Dutton, 2003).
4. (New York: Threshold, 2009).

consider how those we deem immoralists could still possibly be moral (or at least not *completely* immoral).

How Do You Talk to Stupid People?

It is a well-known fact that atheism has long suffered from an image problem. Indeed, chapter ten will deal squarely with this issue when we consider carefully Ted's aversion to atheists. But atheists are aware of the problem and have gone some distance toward attempting to redress it. One notable attempt came in 2003 when Paul Geisert and Mynga Futrell coined the term *bright* as a more positive way to describe those who assent to a naturalistic view of the world (meaning that they reject any supernatural or mystical element). The move was a wry attempt to shift from the negative focus on what atheists deny (notably the existence of God and an afterlife) to a positive focus on what they affirm (an optimistic view of human potential, awe in the mystery and beauty of the universe, especially as it is explicated in science, and a few other niceties).[5] While a number of atheists enthusiastically adopted their rebranding as "brights," others saw a dark cloud with the silver lining. As atheist Chris Mooney rightly worried, "How could anyone hear the label 'bright' and think anything *but* that atheists were claiming to be smarter than everyone else?"[6] Mooney rightly worried that the term could easily backfire, leading a skeptical public to conclude not that atheists were particularly bright but rather that they were plain obnoxious.

The defenders of the term *bright*, notably the philosopher Daniel Dennett, sought to defuse these criticisms by claiming that the term

---

5. The main bright website is at http://the-brights.net/.

6. Mooney wisely concludes, "I suspect that what atheists really need is for people to believe that they are likeable, and not so different from everybody else. So perhaps future atheist message crusaders should describe themselves and their brethren as humble, rather than angry or sneering or super smart." "Not Too 'Bright,'" http://www.csicop.org/doubtandabout/brights/.

was never intended to suggest the atheist's intellectual superiority. But it is very difficult to take that disclaimer seriously, particularly when we peruse the actual writings of atheists and other skeptics of religion. In light of the popular new atheistic dichotomy between the enlightened secular illuminati and the unenlightened religious rubes outlined in the last chapter, it is hardly surprising that the introduction of a term like *bright* has been widely interpreted as a dig at the religiously not-so-bright. (Admittedly Dawkins and others leave open the possibility that the religiously devout really are bright and that they persist in their religion because they are *wicked*. But that is certainly not much of a consolation prize.) In addition to the recent writings of prominent atheists like Richard Dawkins, recent pro-atheist films drive the point home. For instance, Brian Flemming's 2005 documentary, *The God Who Wasn't There*, makes the charge that the greatest sin within Christianity is *thinking*. No better is Larry Charles's popular film *Religulous*, which features comedian Bill Maher traveling the globe and interviewing religious people with the apparent end of highlighting their patent absurdities. Evidence such as this lends powerful support to the assumption that calling atheists "brights" leaves the religious person to choose whether they prefer to be "plain dark" (that is, stupidly religious) or "dark deluxe" (that is, wickedly religious).

It is disconcerting to note how frequently atheists actually raise the dark deluxe, wicked theist charge against Christians. Consider for instance the charge that David Mills made in his popular book *Atheist Universe*: "The language used by Christian-apologist writers is deliberately obscure and jargon-filled to create the façade of intellectual respectability."[7] If we think about it, the claim is really astounding. If Mills is to be believed, Christianity's leading apologists are engaged in a massive and systematic attempt to obfuscate the pertinent issues by *intentionally coining obscure and confusing terminology*. It is not simply

---

7. David Mills, *Atheist Universe: The Thinking Person's Answer to Christian Fundamentalism* (Berkeley: Ulysses, 2006), 57.

that the apologists do a poor job of communicating; rather, they are actually intending to deceive others. In this they are no different from a pretentious graduate student who delivers a nonsense seminar paper laden with unnecessarily technical terminology, merely so that he may build his reputation as a profound thinker. And as if that were not bad enough, Mills also criticized former atheists who claimed to have converted to theistic intelligent design theory because of the evidence:

> To me, what is among the most annoying habits of ID's [intelligent design's] writers is their peculiar tendency to plagiarize each other's life stories. Virtually every ID author doles out the identical biographical yarn that, before his awakening to the impeccable logic of Intelligent Design, he was a notorious atheist (e.g., immoral, crude, self-centered). I suspect that such a spiritual rags-to-riches tale goes over well at church revivals and tent meetings. But I have yet to locate a single bit of reliable, independent evidence to corroborate any such personal history of any well-known advocate of Intelligent Design.[8]

Unfortunately, Mills provided no documentation to support these startling claims that apologists collude and fabricate their testimonies. And we wonder what possible evidence he could have for such a fantastic charge. To take one example: Does Mills seriously believe that best-selling apologist and ID defender Lee Strobel *fabricated* his atheism-to-Christianity conversion story? If he has such evidence, he should let the world know. Indeed, in this world of sensational tabloid journalism Mills could probably make some good money by selling the story.

Not surprisingly, Christians have taken issue with the view that their perspective is held because of rank ignorance, stupidity, and/ or evil. When the term *bright* was first coined, Christian writer

---

8. Mills, *Atheist Universe*, 240.

Dinesh D'Souza wrote a scathing reply in the *Wall Street Journal* titled "Not So 'Bright'" in which he complained that "Mr. Dennett, like many atheists, is confident that atheists are simply brighter—more rational—than religious believers. Their assumption is: We nonbelievers employ critical reason while the theists rely on blind faith."[9] Clearly D'Souza did not appreciate the suggestion that Christians are mentally or morally incapacitated. While I sympathize with D'Souza's frustration, it is doubtful that evangelical Christians are much more nuanced when dealing with their own critics. Indeed, truth be known, we are often just as ready to ascribe diagnoses of gross cognitive and/ or moral ineptitude to the atheist, agnostic, humanist, rationalist, skeptic, or freethinker.

It might be helpful at this point to consider a practical, real-world example of how Christian assumptions about the ignorance and/ or immorality of the atheist dissenter play out. A few months ago I read a blog post written by a conservative evangelical. In the post the blogger described how she had been listening to a radio program that featured hosts who prided themselves on entertaining any and all opinions with seriousness and courtesy. It was an open-line call-in show, and a number of people were calling to share their opinions on a wide range of topics. Then a conservative Christian woman called in and made the statement that the world's languages can be traced to the confounding of tongues at the Tower of Babel, as described in Genesis 11. At this point the hosts abandoned their modus operandi of tolerant and courteous engagement and reverted to snickers and mockery. The blogger who was listening to the whole exchange concluded that, inconsistent though the hosts may have been, their hostility was predictable since Christians should *expect* to have their views mocked and held in contempt by the world.

---

9. http://online.wsj.com/article/SB106540510051528700.html.

Note the blogger's assumption that whenever Christians fail to persuade others it is automatically ascribed to the intransigence of the hostile fallen world. Among other things, this is a great way to excuse Christians for failing to present Christian claims winsomely. But even based simply on the blogger's account of the exchange, I found it rather unfair to lay all the blame at the feet of the hosts, as if non-Christians are fated to dismiss any Christian claims with snickering, mockery, and contempt. While these hosts may have failed to show courtesy, this hardly exonerated the caller, who utterly failed to defend her claim that multiple languages originated at a single primal event. If she neglected (or refused) to offer any reasoned defense for a story that strikes many honest people as rather fantastical and mythic, is it really such a surprise that the hosts retreated to the lower road of snickering, mockery, and contempt? If not excusable, such behavior is at least understandable.

If you find that you still have no sympathy with the hosts, then consider a parallel situation in which you were the host and the caller is the adherent of an indigenous religion. In this case the woman calls in and claims that all the languages of the earth originated from a single cosmic egg that exploded out of a great volcano and fell to earth. When it hit the earth, the egg broke into many pieces, with each piece becoming a different language. Imagine that she offered this story as a serious account of the original protolanguages that form the major linguistic groups. As the host, you might be too polite to mock this individual, but you would probably have to struggle mightily not to condescend to her for presenting such an outrageous claim as straight, historical fact. Then imagine that a listener who held to the same religious beliefs blogged afterward about your condescending attitude toward the caller, noting that your skeptical attitude was precisely what believers of this indigenous religion should expect from "the world." I am sure you would find this a bit unfair. Condescending though you may have been, couldn't they appreciate that from your perspective those beliefs appeared to be completely ridiculous and mythical? Surely the caller has an obligation to offer some sort of defense for her claims.

Now back to our main story. This blogger's post attracted a number of critical responses from atheists. While a few of them posted trenchant questions in which they asked the blogger for evidence in support of "the Babel thesis," a number of others appeared to be content with piling on more snickers, mockery, and contempt. Indeed, in at least one case an atheist retorted that the blogger's views were *deserving* of nothing more than mockery. While this was surely an unfortunate attitude, it again seemed to me a predictable response to the "they will hate us because we're faithful" explanation, which really does nothing more than remove the Christian's burden of persuasive argument. As such, it completely forgets Peter's advice to "always be prepared to give an answer to everyone who asks you to give the reason for the hope that you have. But do this with gentleness and respect" (1 Peter 3:15). If we shirk that responsibility by claiming that we are doomed to be misunderstood, we will never grow in understanding and will have nobody to blame but ourselves.

Why Idiots Are Not All That Idiotic

Our four categories—ignorance, idiocy, insanity, and immorality— really reduce to two main charges: cognitive deficiency and moral deficiency. So as we proceed, we will focus in on these two charges. We will begin in this section by considering the viability of charging others with cognitive deficiency (that is, idiocy or its nearby bedfellows, ignorance and insanity). From that point we shall turn in the next section to consider the companion charge of moral deficiency.

It is tempting to think that those who hold beliefs radically different from our own are just plain stupid. The atheistic linguist who encounters the Christian's "Babel thesis" as a serious account of linguistic diversity may be stunned into silence. By the same token, the Christian who learns of the atheistic linguist's belief that human beings emerged through a random, unguided, evolutionary process is equally incredulous. The next question is, How shall we respond to our own incredulity? Should we just sit there, looking stunned at one another? One way to break the silence is through mockery or caricature. For instance, there certainly seems to be some caricature in Del Tackett's description in *The Truth Project* of the atheistic view of the human person as "imago Goo" (as opposed to *imago Dei*, or image of God). Although this is clearly a bald and uncharitable interpretation of the atheist's position, it is rhetorically powerful when delivered to a receptive audience. And rest assured, once the insults have started, the atheist will have an equally lowbrow insult ready to retort to the devout Christian. Perhaps something on the level of "Faithhead! Faithhead!"

Suddenly we find ourselves in a standoff in which both the Christian and her interlocutor are convinced that the other person is crazy, even as each reinforces her perception with a range of caricatures. The only way to break this kind of standoff is by taking the risk of lowering our own rhetorical guns. What if we opted to restrain ourselves from cheap shots and caricatures and instead attempted to understand views that strike us on first blush to be utterly implausible? What would happen if we refused to dismiss our interlocutor as cognitively deficient and instead tried to listen to the other person from "inside" her beliefs, as far as we are able? Even better, what if she then extended the same courtesy to us?

In order to move beyond the lingering suspicion of cognitive deficiency in the other, we need to appreciate the degree to which plausibility and rationality are conditioned by life experience and presuppositions. Richard Lewontin made the point memorably in a critical review of Carl Sagan's book *The Demon-Haunted World: Science as a Candle in the Dark*. In his review, Lewontin took Sagan to task for his simplistic construal of religion as rooted in an irrational, implausible faith that contrasts with the inherently rational and plausible claims of science. Lewontin began by pointing out how manifestly absurd many of the claims of the scientist appear. Consider for instance how the current form of the atomic theory of matter as vibrating packets of energy runs directly counter to our common-sense experience of the world. As Lewontin put it, "Do physicists really expect me to accept without serious qualms that the pungent cheese that I had for lunch is really made up of tiny, tasteless, odorless, colorless packets of energy with nothing but empty space between them?"[10] It may be that the atomic theory of matter is correct, but let us acknowledge that it entails a huge leap away from common sense. Moreover, we are only able to make that leap because we have already accepted a whole range of assumptions about the nature and the status of scientific inquiry, evidence, and theory.

As Lewontin's quote suggests, there is an undeniable tension between the common-sense and scientific views of the world. It is fundamentally mysterious how a particular collection of microscopic vibrating packets of energy could, on the macroscopic scale, be a pungent, creamy slab of cheese, while another collection is a fragrant rose or a musty old book. It would seem that we tolerate this mystery because we grant authority to both common sense and science. But then what about the mysteries of theology? Are those not acceptable for the person who grants authority to theology? This is how Lewontin put it: "What seems absurd depends on one's prejudice. Carl Sagan accepts, as I do, the duality of light, which is at the same time wave and particle, but he thinks that the consubstantiality of Father, Son, and Holy Ghost puts the mystery of the Holy Trinity 'in deep trouble.' Two's company, but three's a crowd."[11] The lesson is that people tend to show tolerance for the mysteries that arise from their beliefs, while being intolerant of the mysteries that arise in the beliefs of others. This reminds me of the parable of the man forgiven a large debt who

---

10. Richard Lewontin, "Billions and Billions of Demons," review of Sagan, *The Demon-Haunted World* in *NY Times Review of Books* (Jan. 9, 1997), 31.

11. Lewontin, "Billions and Billions of Demons," 31.

then turned around to demand a small debt from his neighbor. We readily forgive our own looming mysteries, even as we promptly cry, "Irrationality!" to the most modest mystery in our neighbors.

The point is emphatically not that every view is as reasonable or every mystery as tolerable, as every other. As I have argued, truth is an objective concept that stands apart from our opinions. Isaac Asimov made the point effectively when he observed: "When people thought the Earth was flat, they were wrong. When people thought the Earth was spherical they were wrong. But if you think that thinking the Earth is spherical is just as wrong as thinking the Earth is flat, then your view is wronger than both of them put together."[12] In other words, our beliefs or theories about the world are bound to be more or less correct. Consequently, the biggest mistake of all is to fall into the relativist's blunder of thinking every view is as good as every other. But even if we reject crass relativism, we should also concede that in most cases of disagreement the winner is not as obvious as in the spherical-earth versus flat-earth disagreement. And so we should recognize that every perspective or theory will pose mysteries, suffer some explanatory gaps, and leave some remaining questions.

In sum, the lesson is that we need to keep an eye on our own mysteries and difficulties as surely as we focus on those of our interlocutors. (Back to the confirmation bias.) As a result, it is simply inappropriate to attempt to write off people we disagree with as holding their particular views out of some admixture of ignorance, idiocy, and/or insanity. Instead, we ought to concede in principle that every person could become a legitimate partner in ongoing conversation, no matter how strange his or her beliefs might appear to us at first blush. It may be that some of those beliefs, like a flat earth, will not get far at all. But others might have much to be said for them. And a few of them might even win us over.

---

12. Isaac Asimov, *The Relativity of Wrong* (New York: Doubleday, 1988), 226.

Imagine how this commitment to finding the truth (or at least plausibility) in the other person would have transformed the regrettable exchange we considered above between the evangelical Christian and atheists over the Babel thesis. Had the atheists conceded that this story is plausible against a particular background set of assumptions (e.g., the acceptance of biblical authority and inspiration), they could have set aside their debilitating incredulity and engaged the caller more constructively. In turn, this would have defused the blogger's assumptions that faithful Christian witnesses are bound to be mocked by an unbelieving world. And with the caller's defenses down, the hosts could have reasonably inquired as to the availability of evidence by which this claim could be tested apart from the confession of the Bible as an authoritative text. For her part, the blogger should have reminded herself that the atheists' position is not necessarily a sign of insolent rebellion. From their perspective her beliefs really do appear mythical. No doubt, had both sides extended a little more charity, the consequence would have been much less heat and a lot more light.

Why Immoralists Are Not All That Immoral

At this point we turn from the precincts of cognitive deficiency (ignorance, idiocy, and insanity) to the somber charge of moral deficiency. For those of us who would sooner be considered a pious fool than an evil genius, this may be the most disturbing charge of all. One reason it is so worrisome comes from the fact that people respond to views deemed immoral not simply with condescension but with contempt. As a result, the immorality charge involves a judgment against character that goes much deeper than the guilt of inexplicable ignorance.

Consider first a person who holds a belief that is merely implausible. Imagine a college freshman named Alby who has come from a fundamentalist church in the Nevada desert in order to attend his first semester at the University of Nevada, Las Vegas (UNLV). Since Alby has been taught from birth that the earth is flat, he becomes very distraught when, in a lecture on the hydrologic cycle, he first learns that the earth is a sphere. This leads him to interrupt the baffled professor (to the considerable amusement of the other students): "But my pastor said that the rain comes when water in the oceans above leaks through holes in the firmament!" Although Alby's view is clearly false, and has been known to be so for several centuries, surely the proper initial response to Alby's adherence to this belief is not one of *contempt:* a young man who has been kept ignorant of widely known facts about the natural world is owed our sympathy, not our disdain.

The situation becomes more serious when we come to the realm of immoral belief. Imagine Buzz, a young man who has come from a white supremacist compound in the Nevada desert, in order to attend his first semester at UNLV. Since Buzz has been taught from birth that African Americans are intellectually inferior to Caucasians, he becomes very distraught when, in the same lecture on the hydrologic cycle, the professor makes a glowing reference to the work of *African-American* astrophysicist Neil deGrasse Tyson. Racist Buzz blurts out in front of a shocked class: "But my science teacher said that black people don't know anything about science because they're all dumb!" Whereas Alby might receive some sympathy—poor guy, raised to think the earth is flat!—Buzz would likely get a lot less. Although he too could be seen as a victim of his own deeply flawed epistemic community, we still naturally conclude that morally speaking, Buzz's error is deeper than Alby's—and so is our resulting judgment of him.[13]

Fortunately we can set Buzz and his racism to one side, for in most cases the immorality charge is not directed at the beliefs people hold but rather at *the way they hold their beliefs*. That is, even if the

---

13. Why exactly do we judge Buzz differently from Alby? One explanation traces to the idea of a moral law written on the heart (e.g., Romans 2:14–15). Thus, irrespective of what his epistemic community said, Buzz knew that all people are equal and thus his adherence to his community's racism constituted a culpable denial of this innate or natural knowledge.

beliefs are not themselves immoral, nonetheless, the way the person is holding them is. Consider those people Richard Dawkins lamented because they still reject Darwinian evolution. Dawkins suggested that they might reject evolution because they are wicked. I don't think Dawkins meant to claim that the doctrine of special creation and other alternatives to Darwinian evolution are wicked beliefs *in themselves*. Rather, it seems to me that the charge of wickedness relates to the way they are holding their beliefs: namely, despite the overwhelming evidence to the contrary. In this case it is not the belief itself that is immoral, but rather the person's recalcitrance in retaining it. To illustrate the subtle way that wickedness can enter the way we believe, let's return to our distraught flat-earth student Alby. When Alby first interrupted his professor he was not contemptible so much as pitiable. However, let's pick up the story from this initial confrontation over the hydrologic cycle. From that point Alby's professors kindly provided him with ample evidence to establish the spherical form of the earth, and Alby repeatedly refused to consider any of it. He started out simply overwhelmed as he struggled to keep his bearings in light of a significant upheaval in his worldview. But over several months his confidence was restored (though, alas, not with any good evidence) as his initial, naive flat-earthism morphed into a more sophisticated and worldly-wise flat-earthism. At the same time, the way that Alby held his belief became increasingly immoral, as his refusal to engage his professors openly was fueled by a growing belligerence, wicked jealousy, and prideful desire to show himself the intellectual superior of his UNLV professors. In addition, Alby began to derive a certain satisfaction from being a controversialist. Though Alby's belief was initially held out of a nonculpable ignorance of the facts, he has retained that belief through an increasingly rebellious spirit that has become contemptible indeed.

Our reflection on Alby the wicked flat-earther should provide the occasion for turning the tables on ourselves. He may have managed to convince himself that he is a crusader for truth, even though his deeper motivations may arise from nothing more than a competitive spirit and a prideful sense of intellectual superiority. But then the same often goes for us. How often do we "stay the course," persisting in a belief despite the evidence because of a subtle rebellion, a stubborn refusal to admit that we were wrong, or a pathetic attempt to assert our own identity? It may sound overly dramatic to trace our determination to hold a position despite all comers as an instance of wicked pride, but we cannot foreclose the possibility that this might sometimes explain our resolve. Pure though we may think our intentions to be, the primal sin of pride is always lurking in the nearby bushes.

Coda

The historian Howard Zinn fought as a bombardier in World War II. While he was initially elated to read of the bombing of Hiroshima because it signaled an end to the war, he later reflected: "I had no idea what the explosion of the atomic bomb had done to the men, women, and children of Hiroshima. It was abstract and distant, as were the deaths of the people from the bombs I had dropped in Europe from a height of six miles; I was unable to see anything below, there was no visible blood, and there were no audible screams."[14]

In wartime it pays to keep the enemy at a distance, for it is much easier to hate and kill those we do not know. But when we come close and stare into the faces of those we are preparing to bomb, when we learn their names and discover their passions, when we realize (as Sting sang of the Russians) that they love their children too, then our confidence in the unqualified rightness of our cause and methods begins to diminish. The same dynamic is operative in disagreement and argument. Once we come to know our intellectual opponents,

---

14. Zinn, "Just and Unjust War," in *Passionate Declarations: Essays on War and Justice* (New York: HarperCollins, 2003), 96.

we can no longer dismiss them as cognitively and/or morally deficient. Indeed, we may discover that they are sometimes more intelligent and moral than we are. And here we come to an ironic conclusion that listening to our enemies just may be the best way to destroy them. "*Destroy?*" you reply. "*A rather ironic conclusion to an irenic chapter, isn't it?*" No, not the way I mean it, for as Abraham Lincoln observed, "Do I not destroy my enemies when I make them my friends?"[15]

---

15. Cited in William Barclay, *The Gospel of Luke* (Louisville, KY: Westminster John Knox Press, 2001), 155.

6

THIS CONVERSATION **COULD CHANGE** YOUR LIFE

Let me set the scene. You are a very successful Christian writer and speaker with a loving family, a supportive church, and a burgeoning ministry around the world. Millions look to you for guidance and wisdom, hanging on to every word you write and speak. Over the years your ministry has brought countless people comfort while strengthening their conviction in the truth of Christianity. Now you have just finished a successful book tour for your latest bestseller and are boarding a red-eye flight back home. As you move toward your seat, you notice an elderly man seated just across the aisle. He sits quietly, studying you intently as you put your suitcase in the overhead bin and flop into your seat. At that point he leans across the aisle, and, instead of the anticipated request for an autograph, he declares: "I have something to tell you. But be warned, if you listen with an open mind, what I have to tell you will cause you to lose your faith." While your first reaction is to decline his offer politely as the ramblings of somebody who is mentally unstable, something about his deadly serious demeanor unsettles you. As you stare back at his intense countenance, the thought begins to germinate that just possibly he might indeed be able to say something that would cause you to lose your faith. With that thought lingering in the back of your mind, what would you say in response to him? Would you want to hear what he has to say, knowing that this could indeed lead to the dissolution of your ministry, thereby causing innumerable people (include those you love most) untold shock and grief? Or would you politely decline and do your casual best to turn your attention to the in-flight magazine?

As we ruminate over this dilemma, think back to the introduction of the book where we met poor Sol and witnessed his lamentable declaration that he would sooner have God (or his beliefs about God) than the truth. If we don't want to be like Sol, if we are convinced that we must strive to know the truth, whatever it may be, then we might think that the right response in the present case would be to invite the old man to share his information. After all, how could we choose a burgeoning career over learning the truth? But things may not be quite that simple. Note carefully what the man said: "What I have to tell you will cause you to lose your faith." He *never* said that what he has to say is *true* or *probably true* or that it *ought* to cause you to lose your faith; he only said that it will. So then, before deciding to listen to what the man has to say, wouldn't you want to know whether it constituted a good reason to surrender your faith? After all, it would be a terrible tragedy if the man told you something false or misleading that led you to abandon the true faith.

So what is a self-confessed pursuer of the truth to do? Should you invite the old man to continue? This dilemma serves as an allegory for the event of engaging in open and critical dialogue with another person. Whenever we engage with another person honestly in such a way that we present our own opinions as well as listening to the opinions of others, we are placing ourselves at the risk of the unknown. It could lead to our converting the other, but, for all we know, it could just as well result in the other converting us. That is the final, unsettling consequence of a character formed by truth. We just never know which conversation could ultimately change our lives. It could be that incidental encounter with an agnostic at a bus stop, or that late-night conversation with a young Muslim on a college campus, or the brief exchange with an eccentric elderly man on a red-eye flight. If we resolve always to seek the truth and thereby to move out from behind the ramparts of our secure binary oppositions and onto the vulnerable field of open dialogue, and if we refuse to marginalize our intellectual opponents as cognitively or morally deficient, we face risk with every conversation. Though we could lead them into truth, they could also lead us into error. And if we add that they might also lead us into truth, we should admit that we could also lead them into error. In short, every real conversation is an exercise in stepping into the unknown.

If we are honest, we must admit that this presents something of a dilemma. If we thought that the truthful character is guaranteed to find true beliefs, we had better recognize now that there are no guarantees. This revelation—that despite our best efforts we could still fail to get the truth—could lead us to ask whether truth-seeking dialogue really is worth the risk. The short answer is: we may not have much choice. In order to unpack that point, let's consider a famous mountaineering illustration given by the philosopher William James:

> Suppose that you are climbing a mountain and have worked yourself into a position from which the only escape is by a terrible leap. Have faith that you can successfully make it, and your feet are nerved to its accomplishment. But mistrust yourself and think of all the sweet things you have heard the scientists say of the *maybes*, and you will hesitate so long that, at last, all unstrung and trembling, and launching yourself in a moment of despair, you roll in the abyss.[1]

---

1. William James, "The Will to Believe," in *The Will to Believe and Other Essays in Popular Philosophy and Human Immortality* (Mineola, NY: Dover, 1956), 59.

Think about the dilemma that James described. We need to get down the mountain, but the only way to do so is by leaping across the crevasse. Our dilemma now lies in knowing that we *might* not make it and yet also knowing that our best hope of survival is found in gathering our courage and making the leap anyway. Though the risk will always remain, we know that ultimately we must leap, for we do not have the option to remain on the mountain forever.

Think of the leap over the crevasse as the conversation that we could have with that agnostic waiting at the bus stop, the Muslim on the college campus, or the elderly man sitting across the aisle on a red-eye flight. With each encounter we have a choice: Shall we "jump" by engaging in a real conversation, or shall we refuse by remaining safely with our entrenched beliefs? To refuse to jump in perpetuity leaves us high on the slope, locked in our binary categories, and far from the disciplines that mark us as people of truth. To refuse to converse will kill a truthful character as surely as remaining high on the mountain will kill a healthy body. And so we jump by engaging that agnostic, the Muslim, and the elderly man on the plane. Each conversation, like each leap across a crevasse, poses a risk. But if we aim to be conformed to the truth in our character, each is a risk we must take.

The goal of this chapter is to explore the dynamic that arises when we opt to make that leap by entering into the risk of a vulnerable conversation. To that end, we shall begin with some words on the nature of love and the love of the truth. Next, we shall explore two dimensions of the love of truth, first as it comes through rigorous argument with others and second as it comes through a careful and attentive listening to others. We shall conclude with a vivid real-life illustration of the risk of vulnerable dialogue with the unsettling story of missionary Daniel L. Everett, converted by the very people he went to save.

Love, Truth, and Loving the Truth

It is a matter to be lamented that so many people seem to derive their notion of romantic love from pop songs and Hollywood films. Surely one of the worst offenders in this regard is director James Cameron's film *Titanic*, which centers on the tumultuous romance that unfolds between Rose DeWitt Bukater (Kate Winslet) and Jack Dawson (Leonardo DiCaprio) in the final days before the sinking of the good ship *Titanic*. The film opens in the present day with Rose, now one hundred years old, being brought out to a salvage ship that is searching the wreckage of the *Titanic*. This setting provides the background for Rose to reminisce on that fateful romantic voyage from the first pivotal moment when Jack saved her from committing suicide to the last moment when he slipped beneath the waves of the icy North Atlantic.

Despite the fact that *Titanic* packed cinemas with swooning teenage girls, the film had little if anything to do with true love. Just think about the premise: a centenarian is still fantasizing about the twenty-year-old man she had had a brief fling with eight decades before. What's romantic about that? The fact is that Rose never really knew Jack. She certainly never saw him grow old and lose his hair in some places (while growing it in others). Nor did she ever see him get age spots and varicose veins, expand in the midsection, become debilitated from arthritis, suffer from colorectal cancer, and finally succumb to dementia. All she has is a fantasy of a young man that has apparently served over the years as a convenient periodic respite from the sometimes unpleasant reality of her real husband and family. Far from being true love, this is an unhealthy, regressive infatuation. Exciting though the fantasy may be, real love is found not in a constructed image from long ago but rather in the commitment that sustains us through the trials of receding hairlines, overdrawn bank accounts, expanding waistlines, and devastating medical diagnoses. Perhaps Rose's attraction to Jack could have developed into love, but, alas, we suspect that *that* sort of movie would not have sold nearly as many tickets. True love, it would seem, is just not that romantic.

A good place to begin thinking about the nature of true love is by considering the familiar marital vows: "to have and to hold, from this day forward, for better or for worse, for richer or for poorer, in sickness and in health, to love and to cherish, until death do us part." Had the *Titanic* completed its voyage and Rose and Jack continued dating, she would have had her original attraction tested many times over. No doubt within a year her image of Jack would have become much more tarnished and realistic than those heady days of shallow infatuation on the deep Atlantic. However, if Rose truly came to love Jack, and not simply her ruddy and handsome image of him, she would count this a good thing. She would want to know the truth of this man, difficult though that truth would sometimes be.

The old marital vows that provide a solid template for those who desire to know the truth of a person also provide a good basis for seeking to know the truth generally. Those who strive to have their characters formed by truth desire to unite with reality in much the way one person commits to unite with another. Just as infatuation is arrested at the surface image, so it is with our infatuation with reality: there too we can "love" our image more deeply than the reality that lies beyond. The confirmation bias, the binary opposition, the marginalization of the other as stupid or wicked—all these reflect an infatuation with reality only insofar as it corresponds with our beliefs. This is what marital vows look like when we shift the context from the truth of a romantic consort to the truth of reality: Do you take reality, to have and to hold, from this day forward, for better or for worse, for richer or for poorer, in sickness and in health, to love and to cherish, until death do us part?

The goal of these vows, whether they are directed at another person or reality itself, is the desire for truth. We proclaim our love of reality, but what happens when our beliefs about reality are challenged and shaken? Did we ever really want to know the truth, or will we retrench to the delusions of an infatuation?

Truth Is Worth an Argument

Picture a couple celebrating their fiftieth wedding anniversary. At the reception the master of ceremonies notes with great admiration that in all their years the couple have never had an argument. You would probably assume that this is the mark of a great marriage. But what if they never had an argument because they have never talked about anything more substantial than the weather? And what if they had actually decided never to move their marriage beyond the shallows of trivial talk for fear that they might actually disagree about something and end up arguing? Surely we would never consider a superficial marriage like this as something to be emulated. We would want to tell this couple that there is nothing intrinsically wrong with argument: indeed, argument is often the very path toward truth in a marriage as much as in our basic understanding of reality and interaction with others.

If we are to make sure that this point resonates as it should, we should say a bit more about the notion of argument. This is important, for I suspect that many people share with that couple married fifty years a rather narrow conception of argument as that unfortunate occasion when people get angry, clench their fists, and raise their voices. But, in point of fact, there is no essential connection between anger and argue. The verb *to argue* comes from a Latin word meaning "to make clear" or "to demonstrate." Even more interestingly, the word derives its root from *arg*, meaning "to shine." So the essence of argument is found neither in anger or aggression, nor for that matter in obfuscating rhetoric or clever sophistry. Rather, in its lofty essence, *to argue is to shine*, to demonstrate or make something clear to another. It is the admission of significant disagreement on a particular issue and the attempt to make clear why we hold the view we do with the intent of persuading others to hold the same view. (Sometimes people have another motivation for arguing: to make themselves look smart and their opponent dumb. That is a rather less noble motivation.) In addition, since we have rejected the marginalization of the other as stupid or wicked, we assume that the other person is aiming at the same noble goal.

Recently I published a journal article critiquing the views of a fellow Christian. This prompted yet another Christian to e-mail me, not to take issue with the content of my argument, mind you, but rather to protest the very notion of criticizing a Christian brother. The assumption seemed to be that Christians should show an outward harmony much like the couple married fifty years that had resolved only to talk about the weather. But this certainly was not Jesus' attitude. He *never* passed up a good argument whenever an important issue of truth was at stake. At the same time, he never treated argument as an end in itself. Rather, argument was always the tool to allow the truth to shine forth. As a result, it should be no surprise that Jesus spent a significant amount of his time arguing (and making some people very angry). Jesus was always ready to confront hypocrisy, and more than once his deft analysis left his critics gnashing their teeth in frustration. Regardless, he always spoke the truth without apology: "Woe to you, teachers of the law and Pharisees, you hypocrites! You are like whitewashed tombs, which look beautiful on the outside but on the inside are full of the bones of the dead and everything unclean" (Matthew 23:27). The cynic might observe that Jesus had not read Dale Carnegie's *How to Win Friends and Influence People*. However, Jesus wasn't interested in winning friends at the expense of bringing people to truth.

Jesus did not force the unwilling Pharisees to confront their own confirmation biases. But he did expose their biases with a lightning logic and masterful argument. Consider his debate concerning paying taxes to Caesar. The starting point of the discussion is the Pharisees' desire not to get at the truth, but to trap Jesus (Matthew 22:15). As a result, they had already failed in the first essential step since their goal was not truth but rather vindication. And so they laid their trap: "Is it right to pay the imperial tax to Caesar or not?" (v. 17). Jesus was surprisingly direct in his response, calling them hypocrites and asking them why they were trying to trap him. But he did not leave it at that, for his argument then unfolded to shine a light on their hypocrisy. With that he requested a coin and asked them to tell him the image and inscription on the coin. Once they gave the predictable reply "Caesar's," he gave his famous response: "Give back to Caesar what is Caesar's, and to God what is God's" (v. 21). A classic case of steering between the horns of a genuine dilemma.[2]

Time and again Jesus laid out bracing argument to back up his claims. Consider the time when he was in the synagogue on the Sabbath. Knowing that the Pharisees had become hypocrites about the law, such that they would consider even a healing on the Sabbath to be forbidden work, he began by asking a pointed question: "Which is lawful on the Sabbath: to do good or to do evil, to save life or to kill?" (Mark 3:4). With this question Jesus brilliantly set them up, reminding them of the most important dimensions of the law. Then Jesus healed the man with the withered hand (v. 5). And how did the Pharisees respond? Did they admit their own hypocrisy? Far from it. Instead, they dismissed Jesus as a false teacher and initiated a plot to kill him. This regrettable outcome provides a final reminder that even while the goal of argument is to shine forth the truth to others, not every good argument is embraced. Nor is a person willing to concede every bias or hypocrisy that is exposed. But that is not necessarily the fault of the one presenting an argument. If Jesus could not win everyone over, we should not worry if we too fail to do so.

---

2. See Douglas Groothuis, *On Jesus* (USA: Thomson Wadsworth), 26–28.

Truth Is Worth a Listen

In addition to the openness to argue, a healthy marriage also requires the willingness—and indeed the *ability*—to listen. After all, a great argument is of limited use if a person refuses to hear it. As we turn our attention now to listening, we should begin by critiquing the rather undeveloped conception of listening common to many. Popular relationship guru John Gray addressed this question in his bestseller *Men Are from Mars, Women Are from Venus,* where he contrasted men (Martians) with women (Venusians). At one point Gray outlined the case of Tom and Mary to explain how men and women have different understandings of listening. In the illustration Mary returns home from a stressful day at work and begins to recount all her frustrations to her husband. Tom does his best to demonstrate that he is listening and to comfort Mary by offering various solutions to each problem that she raises. But instead of being comforted, Mary becomes more exasperated with every piece of advice Tom offers. At this point Gray stepped in with some wise counsel: "Venusians never offer solutions when someone is talking. A way of honoring another Venusian is to listen patiently with empathy, seeking truly to understand the other's feelings."[3] Tom needs to learn that Mary is not looking for a fixer (the perennial tendency of the Martian) but rather a listener, one who will identify with her problems and offer comfort and support.

When it comes to the discipline of listening, Gray's point about Venusians can be readily generalized. We would all do well to forgo quick responses in favor of a careful and reflective listening to others. It is crucial to understand that listening is not evinced simply by brute auditory stimulation and recall. Listening is much more than being a tape recorder. Rather, listening is an empathetic and even incarnational activity in which we seek to put ourselves in the place

---

3. John Gray, *Men Are from Mars, Women Are from Venus* (New York: HarperCollins, 1992), 22–23.

of another. Tom is listening to Mary not simply when he can repeat her story and offer a solution but when he has truly understood her perspective, including her anger and frustration.

Thinking of listening as incarnational naturally draws us to the concept of hospitality. To be hospitable is to invite another person into your personal space and thereby to make space and time for him or her. With this in mind, it has been said that listening is the highest form of hospitality, and this makes good sense. The word *hospitality* comes from a Latin word meaning "friendliness to guests," and that is what we are doing in careful listening: inviting another into our own space by making room for his or her ideas, perspectives, and experiences. That is indeed true hospitality. But we must always remember that when we do that we make ourselves open to being changed by the other. Once invited into our home, he or she may redecorate.

Sadly, people are probably more often than not less interested in listening than in speaking. Like the Pharisees anxious to trap Jesus, we are often more interested in winning over our opponent rather than in getting at the truth. Consider the university classroom. According to the ideal, the classroom is the place where ideas are exchanged, where truth-seeking arguments are carefully listened to, where people are free to think aloud without fear. But, in reality, the classroom is often a battlefield of jostling personalities and closed opinions. Rather than engaging in an open forum of truth-seeking inquiry, students are often locked in a struggle against their peers (and sometimes even their professor). Henri Nouwen helpfully described the unfortunate dynamic that results:

> A student enters into the discussion without knowing much about the subject to be discussed, but with both a desire to know more about it and a fear of showing his ignorance. As soon as someone states an opinion, the most common reaction is not the internal question: "How can I understand *his* opinion better?" but "What

is *my* opinion?" So, too, does silence often mean more an occasion to prepare an answer than to enter the train of thought of the other. And once, two, three, or more opinions are stated the primary concern becomes defense of the chosen position, even when it is hardly worth defending. And so we see how after a while people try to convince themselves and others of ideas that in the beginning they hardly wanted to consider as their own—ideas that were only meant as a hesitant attempt to participate in an exchange of thoughts.[4]

In key respects, the classroom is a microcosm of society. And it also carries over into academia more generally where the struggle initiated in the classroom continues. Hilary Putnam is one rare philosopher who changed his opinions on a number of issues over the years. The interesting thing is that he weathered substantial criticism for changing his views, criticism that, it would seem, is based on the assumption that professors should identify themselves with one particular view (almost like an intellectual "brand") rather than seek the truth openly and without pretension. In response, Putnam once retorted, "A philosopher's job is not to produce a view X and then, if possible, to become universally known as 'Mr. View X' or 'Ms. View X.'"[5] From our earliest days onward to the lofty heights of academic glory, there are pressures to distinguish ourselves for our views rather than in an earnest and honest pursuit of the truth. We must counteract these strong tendencies. The A student is not simply the one with an answer to every question, but the one who quietly and judiciously weighs the options presented through listening. And that carries far beyond the classroom into every aspect of daily life.

---

4. Nouwen, *Creative Ministry* (New York: Image Books, 1991), 8.

5. Putnam, *Representation and Reality* (Cambridge, MA; London: MIT Press, 1988), xii.

Many people have a problem with listening because it seems to be so *passive*. We live in a world in which people are under constant pressure to *do* something. And when we do that, we lose the important dimension of listening and learning. Did you ever stop to ask why, after Jesus rose from the dead, he interacted with his disciples for an additional *forty days* (Acts 1:3) prior to sending them out to proclaim the incredible news of his resurrection? Could it be that Jesus knew well the inestimable importance of that formative period during which the disciples could receive final instructions and be formed through careful listening? Is this not an instructive lesson of how important it is to take the time to listen?

We really need to shake off, once and for all, the assumption that careful and extended listening is doing nothing, because it is in fact a deeply challenging discipline that involves an extraordinary level of control. Consider as an illustration the following story from Zen Buddhism. Long ago a shogun broke into a Buddhist monastery. He then tore through the monastery, slaughtering monks left and right without mercy, until at last he entered the room of the Buddhist master. As the shogun walked up with his large sword smeared with blood, the Buddhist master sat serenely on the floor. After waiting a minute for his seething presence to be acknowledged, the shogun shouted, "Do you realize that I could cut your head off in a moment, and you're just serenely sitting there?" Without missing a beat the Buddhist master replied: "Do you realize that you could cut my head off in a moment, and I'm just serenely sitting here?" The thing that makes this story so powerful is the slow realization that the master is not being passive in light of the shogun's attack. On the contrary, by sitting quiescently on the floor he is exercising an enormous constraint and control. Indeed, from one perspective he is demonstrating a power that outmatches even that of the shogun, whether the barbarian recognizes it or not. Real listening is like this: it is not mere passivity or inactivity, but rather an awe-inspiring power to sit quietly and take in the presence of the other. The world sorely needs this kind of hospitality, and so we would do well to exercise it more often.

The Conversation That Changes Your Life

I could close the chapter with an inspiring reflection on an encouraging case in which argument and listening led to the conversion of a person to Christianity. But instead, to keep us soberly aware of the stakes involved with the pursuit of truth, I am going to close with a rather more sobering case where incarnational listening led a person away from Christianity and thus, I believe, away from the truth.

First, let's think how Christians generally approach the challenge of listening to those of other religions and cultures. Let's say that Ted wants to evangelize the young Hare Krishna man working at the store next to his sporting goods shop. His first stop would be to head down to the local Christian bookstore, where he would pick up a copy of *Dickson's Bible Guide to the Eastern Cults,* a handy resource by a self-described "cult expert" that handily dispenses with the "Hare Krishna cult" in a slim, eight-page chapter and one fold-out reference chart. An example of incarnational listening, do you think? Perhaps before we answer we should flip things around for a minute. Consider that you're a Christian working at a store in India and that the Hare Krishna sporting goods store owner wants to evangelize you. How would you feel when you learned that he had studied up on Christianity by reading an eight-page chapter in a book called *Deepak's Bhāgavata Guide to the Western Cults?* I bet that you would consider that a grossly inadequate way to "dispense" with Christian beliefs. But then why do we find it an adequate way for Ted to deal with the Hare Krishnas? Listening as a real exercise in hospitality involves the invitation of the other into our household of belief, and that means really listening to him or her so that we may truly understand.

The illustration of the old man on the plane flight reminds us that incarnational listening has no guarantees. Indeed, it always carries with it the risk of conversion. We find a riveting example of this risk in Daniel L. Everett's memoir, *Don't Sleep, There Are Snakes*. The book chronicles Everett's experiences as an SIL missionary and translator to the Pirahã people of the Amazon. However, the final chapter tells of the role the Pirahã played in Everett losing his faith. Time and again as he made his best evangelistic efforts, Everett discovered that they had not failed to understand the gospel but rather that they simply were not interested in it. And sometimes Everett's efforts had the opposite effect from what he intended. For instance, when he described the role his stepmother's suicide had played in his conversion, the Pirahãs began to laugh: "She killed herself? Ha ha ha. How stupid. Pirahãs don't kill themselves."[6] And after Everett translated the Gospel of Mark the only part that garnered their interest was the beheading of John. Nothing seemed to work. Increasingly, the task of converting the Pirahã seemed to Everett to be more and more futile. His growing doubts were fed by the recognition that missionaries had attempted to reach these people for two hundred years and that there was no evidence that all that labor had converted even one person.

At the same time that Everett found his own arguments as a Christian missionary coming up short, he also found that listening to the Pirahãs was shaking his own Christian faith. For one thing, he was impacted by their undeniable sense of contentment: they simply showed no need for the gospel; they had no God-shaped hole that he could fill. Augustine's heart may have been restless until it found God, but that did not seem to be the experience of the Pirahãs. This led Everett to question why he was trying "to convince a happy, satisfied people that they are lost and need Jesus as their personal savior."[7] Why try to create in others the need to convert to Christianity when they were already perfectly content with their own beliefs? In short,

---

6. Everett, *Don't Sleep, There Are Snakes: Life and Language in the Amazonian Jungle* (New York: Pantheon, 2008) 265.

7. Everett, *Don't Sleep, There Are Snakes*, 266.

Everett was having the same kind of existential crisis as a refrigerator salesperson living among the Eskimo.

At the same time that Everett found himself with increasing admiration for the Pirahãs' contentment, he was also drawn to aspects of their worldview. Everett discovered that one of the challenges in attempting to persuade the Pirahãs came from their reluctance to believe in anything they could not themselves experience. Since the Gospels spoke of a man who had lived two thousand years ago, they would not believe in him. "The immediacy of experience principle means that if you haven't experienced something directly, your stories about it are largely irrelevant."[8] Rather than view this position as unduly restrictive and unjustified, Everett became increasingly convinced that it was admirably rigorous in its commitment to verifiable evidence: "Creation myths are no match for this demand for evidence."[9] Increasingly Everett came to believe that the faith-based worldview he held could not be justified: "Religious books like the Bible and the Koran glorified this kind of faith in the nonobjective and counterintuitive—life after death, virgin birth, angels, miracles, and so on. The Pirahãs' values of immediacy of experience and demand for evidence made all of this seem deeply dubious."[10] As a result, by the late 1980s Everett had lost faith in God and all things supernatural in favor of a naturalistic worldview focused on the principle of utility: "The Pirahãs are firmly committed to the pragmatic concept of utility. They don't believe in a heaven above us, or a hell below us, or that any abstract cause is worth dying for. They give us an opportunity to consider what a life without absolutes, like righteousness or holiness and sin, could be like. And the vision is appealing."[11]

---

8. Everett, *Don't Sleep, There Are Snakes*, 270.

9. Everett, *Don't Sleep, There Are Snakes*, 270.

10. Everett, *Don't Sleep, There Are Snakes*, 270–1.

11. Everett, *Don't Sleep, There Are Snakes*, 272–3.

Looking back provides little insight into the dynamic of Everett's conversion. After all, he had been a top student at Moody Bible Institute and had often debated thoughtful atheists and agnostics on the streets of North America. Moreover, he had gone to the field with a passion for the gospel and a desire to honor his Lord Jesus Christ as a missionary with rigorous training as well as substantial psychological and spiritual testing. And yet, once in the Amazon jungle, of all places, a "primitive" people shook Everett's deepest beliefs to the core. Nothing in advance provided a warning that this would occur.

I find Everett's reasons for adopting Pirahã pragmatism to be underwhelming, to say the least. But let that be a lesson to us of the risk of listening: when we do so, we don't always make the best decision. From a Christian perspective, Everett's story is a sad one since he surrendered Christian truth for an ultimately false worldview built on pragmatism. But surely this does not mean that SIL should pull its missionaries back into the colonial compound in order to ensure that the "savages" don't convert any more missionaries. When you listen, there is always the risk of assimilation, sometimes for good reasons (for instance, if you're wrong) and sometimes not; but that doesn't mean we have a choice: we have to leap. We just shouldn't be naive when we do.

Coda

So we are left with a dilemma, for when we enter into open dialogue and listening, we risk losing the truth and have no guarantee that we shall gain it. So what do we do with the agnostic waiting at the bus stop, the Muslim on the college campus, the elderly man sitting across the aisle on a red-eye flight, and the Pirahã man in the Amazon forest? If we are serious about truth, we must leap. But is there any consolation before we make this dangerous leap? I propose that we defer to Martin Luther, who offered some famous advice when contemplating another dilemma. What do we do with the fact that we seek to follow Christ even as we know that we will undoubtedly face imminent defeat in the face of temptation and sin? Luther gave the following advice: "If you are a preacher of grace, then preach a true and not a fictitious grace; if grace is true, you must bear a true and not a fictitious sin. God does not save people who are only fictitious sinners. Be a sinner and sin boldly, but believe and rejoice in Christ even more boldly, for he is victorious over sin, death, and the world."[12]

Might I suggest similar advice for our present dilemma? If we are serious about pursuing truth, we must leap boldly into conversation in pursuit of the truth while keeping our eyes on Christ, the perfect embodiment of truth. Even as Christ saw with clarity the distinction between his Father's kingdom and that of the Devil, he warned the rest of us about our own frequent inability to see it. And while he assessed with perfect clarity the heart of every person, he never resorted to the distortions of simplistic judgments. If he became incarnate for us, can we not dare to become incarnate for the people we meet every day?

---

12. Cited in Gene Edward Veith Jr., *A Place to Stand: The Word of God in the Life of Martin Luther* (Nashville: Cumberland House, 2005), 163.

7

NOT ALL LIBERAL CHRISTIANS ARE HERETICS

I t was with great sadness that conservative Presbyterian theologian J. Gresham Machen watched his beloved Princeton Seminary, once the bastion of Calvinistic orthodoxy in North America, slowly morph into a liberal institution. Despite the seemingly insurmountable odds, Machen valiantly fought the battle for old Princeton until he was finally forced to concede defeat in 1929, at which point he left his beloved school in order to help found a new bastion of orthodoxy at Westminster Seminary. In order to appreciate Machen's passionate battle against liberalism, we need to understand what he believed was at stake, and that is fittingly captured in the title of his 1923 book, *Christianity and Liberalism*. As the title implies, Machen believed the new liberalism that was infiltrating university-based seminaries like Princeton to be utterly alien to the Christian gospel. Machen's passion was rooted in the fact that liberalism was not a more liberal form of Christianity but rather a competing religion that sought to replace the gospel of Christ with a set of abstract universal principles. In Machen's view, "liberal Christianity" was no closer to Christianity than Islam or Mormonism, and the sooner the church recognized this fact, the better.

The liberalism that Machen rejected so vociferously was memorably summarized in Adolf von Harnack's influential 1901 book, *What Is Christianity?* While the term *liberalism* has a broader meaning today than it did in Machen's age, for Christian conservatives the exceedingly negative pall remains, with *liberal* often being considered tantamount to *heretic*. And that is serious because the word *heretic* carries with it connotations of fatal doctrinal error as well as questionable moral character. This notion that heresy is closely associated with doctrinal and moral error is ancient, tracing back to second-century interpretations of the New Testament character Simon Magus. Simon appears in Acts 8:9–25 as a magician in Samaria who saw his popularity plummet like a chocolatier at a diet convention with the arrival of Philip and the other apostles. Very soon Simon had joined the masses staring on in wonder at the power exercised by Philip, Peter, and John. Utterly taken with this impressive display, Simon foolishly made an offer to cash in on the power of the Holy Spirit, an offer that quickly elicited a sharp rebuke from Peter and, so the text says, a prompt repentance from Simon.

At this point legend takes over as Christian writers beginning in the second century averred that Simon's repentance was not genuine, claiming instead that he stubbornly persisted in his doctrinal and moral corruption. According to one of these legends, Simon traveled to Rome to confront Peter and Paul in a power encounter reminiscent of Saruman squaring off against Gandalf in *The Lord of the Rings*. To begin with, Simon wowed the crowds by ascending into space in a mockery of Christ's ascension. In response, Peter and Paul prayed intently and thereby managed to break Simon's power, causing him to tumble back to the earth and die a grisly death. While the historical merit of this story is certainly doubtful, it provides a window into early Christian attitudes toward those who fell outside legitimate orthodox boundaries. Their doctrinal error was perceived as a blight on their character as much as their minds.

It is therefore not surprising that evangelicals today commonly view liberals and other heretics as wayward in both doctrine and character. Just ask Ted about those Episcopalian liberals at St. Joseph's Church, and his eyes will flash with derision, anger, and sheer incomprehension at a church that welcomes gays (note the little rainbow symbol on their church sign), abortionists, and a bishop who actually expressed doubts about the resurrection in the local Christian newspaper. Though he has never darkened the door of St. Joseph's, Ted wants nothing to do with that steepled Sodom. The sentiments are reflected in the skit that Ted and his friends performed at last year's men's retreat. Called "Sunday at St. Joe's," it came complete with the following mock hymn:

> Our gospel is inclusive.
> (The other one's passé.)
> We welcome all the sexes,
> Transgendered, lesbigay.
> And though we're loudly preaching
> our relevant good news,
> We are a tad perplexed
> by so many empty pews.[1]

Needless to say, Ted and his friends won first prize.

But are things that simple? Are the liberals who fill the pews at St. Joseph's Episcopalian really heretics, corrupt in both doctrine and life? To ask that question forces us to ask another: Just what is a liberal anyway? J. Gresham Machen may have had a clearly defined group in view regarding liberals, but what is our understanding? We can also turn the question around: While Ted is happy to be called a Christian conservative, what exactly does *that* mean? In order for Ted to understand his own conservative identity, it will be helpful for him

---

1. This parody is available at the conservative Anglican website Virtue Online, http://www.virtueonline.org/portal/modules/news/article.php?storyid=4610.

to listen to those Christians who find themselves at home in the space of St. Joseph's. He should consider what they believe as well as why they believe it. Even if listening does not persuade Ted to transfer his membership to the humble little church, it will, in all likelihood, add a much-needed touch of charity and nuance to his view. When he discovers that many liberals are genuine, sympathetic, and principled people, Ted will have to concede that the harsh Simon Magus–styled judgments of their intellectual and moral character are unfair indeed. In fact, Ted might even find that some Christian liberals evince a deeper spirituality than does he. And the same depth might be seen in their understanding of doctrine. Even if he will ultimately reject many of their views, Ted will not be able to deny that they have thought long and hard about the relevant issues. And this will introduce the final challenge as Ted begins to rethink the assumption lying behind the whole discussion that liberal and conservative are two clearly demarcated positions at opposite ends of the theological battlefield. In fact, as we reflect on the questions raised by liberalism buttressed with observations about Christian faithfulness, we will be brought to the point of drawing some serious reflections about the essence of Christian identity.

Hearing a Liberal's Story

A few years ago I was speaking at a convention for evangelical Christian school teachers. During the talk I noted that the doctrine of the Trinity is an essential Christian belief. Afterward a kindly elderly woman came up to me and, after graciously thanking me for my talk, lodged just one note of disagreement: "Not all Christians are Trinitarians," she said with a smile. After asking her a few questions, I discovered that she was a Oneness Pentecostal, a group that divided from the orthodox Assemblies of God denomination in 1917 because of its conviction that Father, Son, and Spirit are not three persons but rather three manifestations of the one-person God. While speaking with this woman did not change my conviction that assent to the triunity of God is an essential mark of Christian identity, it did remind me of the difference between abstract judgments and concrete conversations. That is, it is one thing to offer a general discussion of heresy and heretics, and it is another thing entirely to speak of heresy when an elderly woman is smiling back at you. As I look back, that conversation made two things clear. First, that woman had thought about the concept of God's triunity more carefully than most ortho- dox Christians.[2] And second, she evinced no noticeable signs of moral corruption. So much for tarring her with the brush of Simon Magus. Indeed, in speaking with her, I was reminded of the words of that great nineteenth-century Unitarian minister William Ellery Channing (who also rejected the Trinity) when he observed: "In following this course we are not conscious of having contracted, in the least degree, the guilt of insincerity."[3] It certainly *seemed* that this elderly woman, like Channing, had rejected the doctrine of the Trinity not out of hostility toward the truth but rather in a sincere pursuit of it.

Once we develop relationships with liberals and other heretics, it can be disconcerting to discover how often their beliefs appear to be held in full sincerity. For another example we can turn to the story of New Testament scholar Marcus Borg as relayed in his intriguing book *Meeting Jesus Again for the First Time.* Though he was raised in a con- servative Christian home, in his teen years Borg began to have doubts about the existence of God: "At the end of childhood there began a period, lasting over twenty years, in which, like many, I struggled with doubt and disbelief. All through this period I continued to think that believing was what the Christian life was all about. Yet no matter how

---

2. For a discussion of this oneness view of the Trinity, often called modalism, see my *Finding God in the Shack* (Colorado Springs, CO: Paternoster, 2009), 51–53.
3. Cited in Gary J. Dorrien, *The Making of American Liberal Theology: Imagining Progressive Religion* (Louisville, KY: Westminster John Knox Press, 2001), 25.

hard I tried, I was unable to 'do' that, and I wondered how others could."[4]

It certainly seems that Borg wanted to believe. Consequently, it does not seem plausible to dismiss his doubts as rationalizations to justify rebellion against God. On the contrary, reading his words I am reminded of the man who, desperate for Jesus to heal his son, cried out, "I do believe; help me overcome my unbelief!" (Mark 9:24). Like that man, Borg seemed to be anxious to believe even as he was beset by doubts. Growing up, Borg had always believed that the Bible's testimony was perfectly reliable. Things got worse when Borg learned in his university and seminary that New Testament scholars distinguish between the Jesus of history and the Christ of the church's faith: in other words, Jesus the man who walked on the dusty paths of Judea two thousand years ago was different from what the church claimed. Unfortunately that discovery deepened Borg's crisis of faith. Increasingly he came to see the church's creedal confessions as veils obscuring the Jesus of history rather than windows revealing him. As a result, that historical Jesus, once so familiar, began to disappear into the mists of antiquity.

The discovery that the Christ of faith was doubted by many scholars left Borg with more questions than answers and ultimately forced him to consider whether to leave the faith. After all, how could he revere a Christ he doubted could be known? But there was another possibility: expand his conception of what it means to be a Christian in a way that would be consistent with his doubts. To opt for the latter course would mean embracing a conception of Christianity that was not so heavily dependent on the beliefs Borg found himself doubting. For a number of years Borg wrestled with these two possibilities until in his thirties he underwent a series of mystical encounters that confirmed for him the abiding presence of God. As a result, these

---

4. Borg, *Meeting Jesus Again for the First Time: The Historical Jesus and the Heart of Contemporary Faith* (New York: HarperSanFrancisco, 1994), 17.

experiences provided a modest foundation for his still shaky faith. In light of his continuing doubts over belief, the faith that emerged was rooted not in doctrine so much as in experience and ethics. Looking back a couple of decades after those experiences, Borg reflected: "Now I no longer see the Christian life as being primarily about believing. The experiences of my midthirties led me to realize that God is and that the central issue of the Christian life is not believing in God or believing in the Bible or believing in the Christian tradition. Rather, the Christian life is about entering into a relationship with that to which the Christian tradition points, which may be spoken of as God, the risen living Christ, or the Spirit."[5]

Ask Borg whether he affirms the great creeds of the faith—the Apostles' Creed and Nicene Creed, for instance—and I suspect that at best you will get a shrug of the shoulders. But rather than abandon the faith, Borg answered his doubts by expanding (or changing) the meaning of Christian so as to find a place in the church for his own praxis and experientially based faith. For Borg the heart of Christian faith is found not in doctrinal assent but rather in a life modeled on the perfect life of Christ.

Those of us who do not struggle with Borg's doubts and who are able to affirm a much fuller set of doctrines may be thankful for our greater confidence. But does that mean that there is no room in the church for Marcus Borg or the many similar souls who fill the pews of a St Joseph's on a Sunday morning? If we are to take Borg's own account seriously, we can no more doubt his sincerity than that of the elderly Oneness Pentecostal woman. Borg too seems to be nothing like Simon Magus, who was maniacally opposed to the truth of the gospel. So far as I can see, Borg appears to want to believe even as he struggles with more doubts than most. As a result, it seems to me simply unfair to attempt to construe his struggles of faith as less than

---

5. Borg, *Meeting Jesus Again for the First Time*, 17.

genuine. But then what is the origin of his doubts? One possibility is to think of his doubts as a special thorn in the flesh. We all know about Paul's thorn in the flesh, an unknown affliction that he prayed to be withdrawn. When Paul prayed to Christ that this thorn might be relieved, the reply came that Paul should instead rely on Christ's strength (2 Corinthians 12:7–10). Many other great Christian leaders of history have suffered their own thorns in the flesh. For instance, Martin Luther struggled all his life with doubts about his salvation. In my view, Luther's sincere struggles evince not a fault in character but rather a burden he was given to draw him back to Christ. Is it at least possible that Borg's struggles over doctrines could likewise be *his* thorn in the flesh?[6] And if this is possible, then wouldn't the proper response to Borg's struggles over doctrine be not anger and censure but rather sympathy and encouragement (without condescension, of course)?[7]

I Believe on the Third Day He Rose Again . . . but Must I?

Although I do not know Marcus Borg personally, I have two good reasons to think he is the genuine article. The first is the quality and integrity that come through his writings. The second is the testimony of that towering intellectual pillar of Anglican orthodoxy N. T. Wright. While Wright is widely lauded as one of the premier New Testament scholars in the world, he is also good friends with Borg.[8] In the eye of many evangelicals the problem arises not with the friendship per se

---

6. The fact that some liberal Christians would repudiate this analysis is not especially relevant, for it would still remain possible that others might suffer from a thorn of doctrinal doubt.

7. Heresy undoubtedly has served a valuable function in the church, and we wonder how often God might have allowed a heretic's mistake as a foil to spur the wider church on to greater doctrinal clarity and fidelity. For a suggestive discussion, see Alister McGrath, *Heresy: A History of Defending the Truth* (New York: HarperOne, 2009).

8. Borg and Wright explored their differences in *The Meaning of Jesus: Two Visions*, 2nd ed. (New York: HarperOne, 2007).

but rather with the fact that Wright believes his resurrection-denying friend is also a Christian. This is how he put it in a 2006 interview: "Marcus Borg really does not believe Jesus Christ was bodily raised from the dead. But I know Marcus well: he loves Jesus and believes in him passionately." So then why does Borg not believe? Wright suggested that "the philosophical and cultural world he has lived in has made it very, very difficult for him to believe in the bodily resurrection."[9] Is it possible, as Wright said, that a person could be a Christian and yet reject the resurrection of Christ?

Let's begin to address this question by turning to the Easter season. Just like clockwork, every Easter, popular magazines like *Time* and *Newsweek* find a way to squeeze Jesus onto the cover, typically with a heading that carries a whiff of scandal like "How the Jesus of History Became the Christ of Faith" or "Did Jesus *Really* Rise?" Without fail, these articles are weighted more to hype than substance. But what if a story broke in the media about Jesus that actually had some substance to it? What if some real evidence arose questioning the resurrection of Jesus? That scenario is addressed in Paul Maier's novel *A Skeleton in God's Closet*. In the story well-respected archaeologist and devout Christian Jonathan Weber is working on a dig for the tomb of Joseph of Arimathea when the remains of Jesus Christ are discovered. As you might guess, with this discovery Weber finds his faith coming under severe testing. After all, if Jesus' bones remained in the tomb, then Jesus did not in fact rise from the dead, and this means that a doctrine that has stood at the center of Christian faith for two thousand years is false. As news of the discovery sweeps the globe, it leaves in its wake a sea of deeply confused Christians. However, Weber observes that not all Christians find their faith upended by the discovery: "A Methodist professor said he'd have to do a lot of rethinking. But an

9. See the interview with Jill Rowbotham: "Resurrecting Faith," *The Australian* (April 13, 2006), available at http://www.virtueonline.org/portal/modules/news/article.php?storyid=3903.

Episcopal rector said that finding Christ's remains 'would not affect me in the slightest.' I recall being totally *disgusted* at that response. The one I easily agreed with was a Catholic New Testament professor at St. Louis University who said that he 'would totally despair.' Now, *that* was honest!"[10]

The scenario leaves each reader to ask the same question for himself or herself. Would I be left to do a lot of rethinking like the Methodist professor? Or would I despair like the Catholic professor? And what about the Episcopalian rector whose faith never depended on the resurrection? What sort of faith is *that* anyway?

Let's think about this question more carefully. If Jesus' body were discovered, we would suddenly find ourselves in Borg's shoes (or a pair much like them), needing to decide whether to leave the faith or reinterpret it. There would be good grounds for the first move, given Paul's declaration that "if Christ has not been raised, our preaching is useless and so is your faith" (1 Corinthians 15:14). So if Christian faith without Christ's resurrection is useless, we might as well find something else to believe in. But what? Islam? Deism? Atheism? *Amway*? (Or perhaps a combination thereof?) The more I think about the radically, sweeping implications of walking away from faith altogether, of rejecting everything in Christianity lock, stock, and barrel, the more game I am to consider the second option. The point can be made by considering G. K. Chesterton's commentary on the complex reasons why people hold Christian belief:

> [I]f one asked an ordinary intelligent man, on the spur of the moment, "Why do you prefer civilization to savagery?" he would look wildly round at object after object, and would only be able to answer vaguely, "Why, there is that bookcase . . . and the coals in the coal-scuttle . . . and pianos . . . and policemen." The whole case for civilization

---

10. Paul Maier, *A Skeleton in God's Closet* (Nashville: Westbow, 1994), 258.

is that the case for it is complex. It has done so many things. But that very multiplicity of proof which ought to make reply overwhelming makes reply impossible.[11]

According to Chesterton, in much the same way that our commitment to civilization depends on a multiplicity of factors rather than a single point, so Christian faith also rests on a multiplicity of factors. People are typically not Christians for one single reason but because of a whole variety of factors. For instance, they have experienced God's providential hand guiding their life, they have found inspiration and guidance in the Scriptures, they have had great Christian mentors and models, their nephew was healed of cancer after an all-night prayer meeting, and God saved their marriage. In short, they are a Christian because it provides the most complete, satisfying, and plausible understanding of the human condition, where we came from and where we are going. For these reasons and many others, they could indeed resist the attempt to throw all this away on the condition that one doctrine should come up false, even if it is a doctrine as central as the bodily resurrection of Christ.

And so, when the alternative of rejecting faith is considered, it might seem preferable to retain our Christian faith, even given the discovery of Jesus' body. But is this really a serious possibility? Or would keeping faith under these conditions be like keeping the marriage going after you discover your spouse is a bigamist? That is, as great as all these other things may be, without a resurrection of Christ is there really anything left to save? While I appreciate the reservation here, I think we need to understand the real force of the civilization parallel. To push things further, consider a specific example. I know a missionary who was home on furlough, raising ministry support, and had come up short three hundred dollars a month. Just when

---

11. Chesterton, *Orthodoxy* (1908; Reprint: London: Hodder & Stoughton, 1996), 119.

he was about to give up, having exhausted every possible avenue of support, he received a call from somebody who felt God laying on his heart the need to support him . . . at three hundred dollars a month. (At this time nobody except the missionary's wife knew of their specific financial need.) I refer to an event like this as a "LAMP," which is an acronym for "little amazing moments of providence." Many Christians have experienced LAMPs like this in their lives. Is it so obvious that the discovery of the body of Jesus would persuade people to dismiss all these LAMPs as mere happenstance? Would they really be forced to reject Christianity, kit and kaboodle, as plain false?

As *A Skeleton in God's Closet* unfolds, Jonathan Weber wrestles with this question: Should he surrender his Christian faith altogether, or could he instead adopt a faith like that of the Episcopalian rector?

> [M]aybe Mark Twain was right, Jon finally had to admit to himself. And not only Twain, but all of liberal theology, which had been denying a physical resurrection of Jesus ever since David Strauss and Ernst Renan did so in nineteenth-century Germany and France. Yes, maybe all the higher critics, particularly Rudolf Bultmann, were right all along. The Resurrection never happened, but it was the *faith and belief* that it did that was important. And all his conservative, Lutheran Church–Missouri Synod Sunday school and Bible classes, and all the endless sermons . . . wrong![12]

As unsettling as the thought is, we ought to reflect on Weber's questions. So I ask myself, if Jesus' body were discovered, would I leave the Christian faith altogether, or would I instead adopt a more liberal interpretation of that faith?

Try as I might, I cannot be sure which of these options I would follow. The dilemma recalls the crisis that lies at the center of William

---

12. Maier, *A Skeleton in God's Closet*, 200.

Styron's novel *Sophie's Choice*, where we meet sweet and brooding young Sophie, a survivor of the Nazi concentration camps. As the novel unfolds, we discover that Sophie was forced by a cruel Nazi to choose which one of her two children would live and which would die. How could any parent be asked to make such an unthinkable choice? The popularity of the book and subsequent film (starring Meryl Streep) led to the popularization of the term "Sophie's choice" as a way to refer to any impossible or unthinkable decision. It seems to me that where the Christian faith is concerned, the discovery of Jesus' remains would pose just such a crisis of decision. Do I reject the faith altogether, or do I set aside the centrality of the historic resurrection? It strikes me that this is by no means a straightforward or easy choice. And if it seems presumptuous to judge Sophie for making such a forced decision, it seems also presumptuous to judge a liberal Christian for having made a theological judgment under equally impossible circumstances.

This brings us back to the Episcopalian rector in Maier's novel and the suspect bishop for the diocese of St. Joseph's Church. In the passage cited above where Jonathan Weber contrasts the Methodist professor, Episcopal rector, and Catholic professor, he finds the ease with which the rector accepts the news "disgusting" but considers the Catholic's growing despair "honest." The Catholic professor may indeed be honest, but does that mean that the rector is disgusting? Some liberals may be inexcusably flippant about, and even hostile toward, the doctrines of faith, but does that mean that all are? Perhaps that rector had already passed through his own dark night of the soul some years before and emerged with an integral liberal faith that can handle a nonresurrected Christ. The question of how anybody could call himself or herself a Christian while doubting Christ's resurrection is transformed if we think of these "liberals" as people who have wrestled with a Sophie's choice. If we do not judge Sophie for choosing one child over another in an impossible decision, can we necessarily judge others who have weathered their own Sophie's choice?

There is one significant problem with the argument so far, and I know that were Ted with us he would point it out. Astute amateur apologist that he is, Ted would reject the assumption that, where the resurrection of Christ is concerned, Christians (liberal or otherwise) face anything like a Sophie's choice. Ted has read Lee Strobel's *The Case for Christ*, and he is quite familiar with the excellent historical grounds for the resurrection. So even if *A Skeleton in God's Closet* suggests a possible scenario in which faith would be challenged, that scenario cannot be invoked in defense of liberals like Marcus Borg. I would agree that the available historical evidence strongly favors the resurrection. But the central point at issue here concerns not what the best objective assessment of the data is but rather *whether certain individuals who are neither stupid nor wicked perceive there to be a real crisis with the church's conception of resurrection*. And Marcus Borg seems to constitute just such an example (perhaps, as Wright believes, because of the "philosophical and cultural world" that he accepts). Whatever the genesis of their doubt, these individuals find themselves in much the same place as Jonathan Weber in *A Skeleton in God's Closet* with a genuine crisis of faith.

Let me suggest a way to explore and expand our sympathy for the liberal. It has been said you ought not judge a man till you've walked a mile in his shoes. (Or, if you prefer, you ought not judge a fashionista until you've walked a mile in her four-inch stiletto-heeled pumps.) With that in mind, a little role-playing is always helpful in thinking through these types of issues. And so let's put Ted in the place of Jonathan Weber. Now it is Ted who has been left to agonize over the apparent discovery of Jesus' body in an archaeological dig. Many of Ted's evangelical friends do not yet appear particularly disturbed by the discovery. Some are too busy to worry, occupied as they are with the more mundane matters of shifting mortgage rates and car payments coming due. Meanwhile others are content to put it all back to faith, without giving a second glance to whatever evidence may arise. But Ted has looked at the evidence of the discovery, and he is deeply disconcerted. Ted knows that his friends are chalking up his doubt to a faith weaker than their own. But even so, he cannot shake the sense that this is a genuine crisis of faith and that he has a real obligation to respond. As time drags on, Ted becomes more desperate for a resolution, and so he reads all that he can get on the topic from archaeologists, apologists, and historians. Finally, after several months of agonizing over the discovery, Ted painfully and tentatively concludes that Jesus was *not* bodily resurrected.

But even in this difficult hour, Ted finds himself unwilling (or unable) to walk away from the faith altogether. He simply has too much invested in Christianity; it makes too much sense in so many ways. For one thing, Ted has his own LAMPs that speak of the fundamental truth of the faith. It all began that chilly winter night when that Campus Crusade for Christ worker came out of nowhere and interrupted Ted's suicidal thoughts with the shattering message that Jesus loved him. And then there was the time when Ted came up $876 short on making the payroll at his business, only to find an envelope with that exact amount sitting in his church mailbox. Could he really throw out these LAMPs, and many others, by calling Christianity a big mistake? What if instead Ted found himself ending up one Sunday morning at St. Joseph's with a new humility and an openness to a church that offers a warm pew to doctrinally stumbling disciples like himself? What do you suppose that Ted would then think of his award-winning "Sunday at St. Joe's" skit?

This brings us to the core debate: Is the evidence for the great truths of Christianity such that an honest person cannot consider them carefully and still find him- or herself in doubt? Or is it indeed possible to find ourselves honestly doubting some of these doctrines? If we conclude the latter, then it would seem that we simply cannot adopt the sweeping cognitive or moral judgment of the liberal. Here it needs to be noted that any judgment is complicated by the fact that there is no single threshold of evidence that would convince everybody of a given truth. Some Christians, like the Episcopalian bishop, give up key doctrines like the bodily resurrection of Christ in response to comparatively low thresholds of evidence. Others would require much greater evidence: perhaps bodily remains that clearly evince the marks of crucifixion being discovered in Joseph of Arimathea's tomb. (Evidentially speaking, this is about where Jonathan Weber finds himself.) Still others would retain faith unless further evidence was added to the body, such as additional first-century documentary evidence that revealed a malicious plot among the apostles. (Perhaps this is where Ted would find his threshold.) And finally, a few others (some of Ted's friends included) would never abandon their faith no matter how strong the evidence against it. (Nor is that unwillingness necessarily admirable.) Here then is our question: Which of these evidential thresholds is the proper point at which faith should be abandoned? The fact is that there is no simple answer to this question. But as we wrestle with it, we will begin to see the tension with the very notion of "liberal" and "conservative."

Somebody, Somewhere *Thinks You're a Liberal*

Let's spend some more time reflecting on the fact that people are persuaded by different degrees of evidence. We can begin by observing that the Episcopalian bishop, Ted, you, and I would all react differently to the discovery of evidence that seemed to contradict the historical resurrection of Jesus. In order to illustrate this, let's begin by proposing a belief scale numbered from 1 to 100 in which the numbers correspond to the strength with which we hold a belief. According to the scale, the higher the number assigned to a belief, the more strongly it is held, and therefore the more contrary evidence to the belief would be required for a person to abandon it. We can refer to the number ascribed to a belief as the belief's "conviction score." So a score of 1 marks a belief that would be abandoned on the most minimal counterevidence, while a belief that scored at 100 would never be abandoned under any circumstances. Such a belief would be held with maximal conviction. With all this in mind, consider the following three beliefs:

(a) My neighbor is trustworthy.

(b) 2 + 2 = 4.

(c) Jesus rose bodily from the dead.

If you believe (a), you might grant it a relatively low conviction score (maybe at a 10 or 20), while you would give (b) a very high score (perhaps close to 100). Where on this scale would (c) fall? That depends on the Christian you ask. Some Christians would ascribe this belief a high conviction score, while other Christians would grant it a much lower one. While the Episcopal bishop might grant belief in the resurrection a score of 40, I might place it at a 75, Ted at an 85, and the pope at a 90. If we assume that Christian liberalism is identified with a relatively low (more specifically, an *inappropriately* low) conviction score for Christian beliefs like (c), where should we nonliberals place that threshold of appropriateness? Let's put this another way: Who decides what the appropriate score in each case is? Ask the Episcopalian bishop, and he might place the normative conviction score around 40, whereas I would place it around 75, Ted around 85, and the pope around 90. From this it follows that each one of us is a liberal relative to some people even as we are a conservative relative to others.

Granted, we cannot really rate beliefs in this precise manner, but I merely offer the numbers to clarify the main point that we certainly do hold beliefs with varying degrees of conviction. And if some Christians hold to some doctrines more loosely than do you, others hold them more firmly. But it is not only that Christians vary in their conviction in various beliefs. In addition, Christians vary in the beliefs they hold. While Borg may have once held the belief in Jesus' resurrection with a lower degree of conviction, at present he does not hold it at all. And then there are the "conservatives," or, as they are often called, the "fundamentalists," who tend to hold more doctrines and have higher conviction scores for those they hold. But if you are looking for an absolute, clear definition of conservative or fundamentalist, you will likely be disappointed. As Alvin Plantinga wryly observed, these days the term typically means nothing more than a person who is "considerably to the right, theologically speaking, of me and my enlightened friends."[13] Or within our present context it means anybody who has a cumulative conviction score substantially higher than mine. So here I am with my 75 conviction score for the resurrection, convinced that those who place the threshold much lower are liberals, while those who place it much higher are fundamentalists. When we then apply the procedure to other beliefs, things begin to get complicated. Consider the following belief:

(d) God is a Trinity of three equal but distinct persons.

Though I hold (c) at a 75 conviction score and Ted holds it at an 85, I might hold (d) at an 85 while Ted holds it at a 75. So when you factor that in, which one of us is the liberal, and which one is the fundamentalist? It would seem that it depends on which belief we are concerned with. Apparently with respect to (c) I'll consider Ted a fundamentalist, while he'll consider me a liberal. But with respect to (d) I'll consider Ted a liberal, while he'll consider me a fundamentalist. Perhaps then these scores cancel each other out, resulting in a tie. That raises an interesting question: Is it clear that every belief is of equal import? Let's say that somebody has a low conviction about baptism as a sacrament of the church but a high conviction about the Trinity. How do you add in the fact that the Trinity is more central than baptism? A very difficult question indeed. And that is only to begin addressing the extraordinary complexities. The lesson is not that

---

13. Plantinga, *Warranted Christian Belief* (Oxford: Oxford University Press, 2000), 245.

we should throw out distinctions like liberal and fundamentalist (or conservative) but rather that we need to recognize that *such judgments are always relative to a context*. With that in mind, remember that if you're ever called a liberal, the first question you need to ask is this: *Relative to whom?*

All this leads to a rather strange consequence: while some Christians will think you're a fundamentalist, others will think you're a liberal. (At least they would if they knew all the things that you believe.) Take for instance the following two beliefs:

(e) The Bible is verbally inspired.

(f) The NIV is a good translation.

You might find (e) and (f) to be relatively uncontroversial beliefs for a Christian to hold, but some Christians will consider you a fundamentalist for holding the former, while others like the Baptist King James Version–only advocate Peter S. Ruckman will consider you a raving liberal for holding the latter.[14] So are you a cross-eyed fundamentalist or a bleary-eyed liberal? It depends on whom you ask. I am reminded here of Brian McLaren's provocative definition of orthodoxy as "what God knows, some of which we believe a little, some of which they believe a little, and about which we all have a whole lot to learn."[15]

---

14. Ruckman is infamous for both his penchant for insulting his critics and his claim that the KJV is "advanced revelation," meaning that it is a translation that actually supersedes all Hebrew and Greek manuscripts of the early church and is the definitive English translation for all time.

15. Brian D. McLaren, *A Generous Orthodoxy* (Grand Rapids, MI: Zondervan, 2004), 32.

Christianity as the Life Lived

So far I have been advocating listening to the liberal so as to cultivate a greater sympathy with his or her more abstemious faith. As we do we will begin to realize that liberals are not just "out there"; they are to be found among us, and even in our mirrors. With that in mind we can now explore the relationship between doctrine and Christian identity by asking the following question: If we are all somewhat liberal in our beliefs, then how liberal is just *too* liberal? It is important to note that this focus on belief or doctrine as central to religious identity is a distinctive emphasis of historic Christianity compared to Judaism and Islam, which have tended to emphasize practice over belief.[16] The liberal, at least the Marcus Borg type, would have us begin to question this traditional Christian distinctive. Once we recognize the complications posed by notions like orthodoxy, heresy, conservatism, and liberalism, we might find ourselves with a new sympathy for the characteristically liberal focus on ethical action over doctrinal assent. Could it be that there is actually something to be said for this liberal approach that locates Christian identity primarily in the life lived rather than in the set of doctrines believed?

Not surprisingly, such proposals tend to set off alarm bells for those of a more conservative bent. This is how that stalwart defender of orthodoxy J. Gresham Machen put it: "It is said, Christianity is a life, not a doctrine. The assertion is often made, and it has an appearance of godliness. But it is radically false, and to detect its falsity one does not even need to be a Christian."[17] Perhaps Machen is correct, but it seems to me that the liberal view that places the deepest roots of Christian identity in ethical action at least deserves a closer look. I will

16. See John B. Henderson, *The Construction of Orthodoxy and Heresy: Neo-Confucian, Islamic, Jewish, and Early Christian Patterns* (Albany, NY: SUNY Press, 1998), 12–15.
17. Machen, *Christianity and Liberalism* (1923; reprint: Grand Rapids, MI: Eerdmans, 1956), 19.

seek to give the view a fair shake here by laying out two contrasting responses toward the 1994 Rwandan genocide—those of Christian Elizaphan Ntakirutimana and Muslim Mbaye Diagne—and then asking us to draw our own conclusions. But before we consider their cases, I will set the context by saying a few words about the genocide itself.

The 1994 Rwandan genocide represents the most efficient genocide in the twentieth century, and virtually all of it was carried out with roving militias brandishing primitive farm implements like scythes and knives. Over a three-month period more than 800,000 Tutsis and moderate Hutus were butchered while the international community stood by. The demonically bureaucratic calculus of geopolitics that drove Western complacency was soberly summarized by one US official who brazenly declared that "one American casualty is worth about 85,000 Rwandan dead."[18] As jolting as this is, statistics inevitably look very different on the ground when each number corresponds to a specific corpse. In one case, the executive assistant of Romeo Dallaire (commander of UN forces) arrived too late to help those hiding in a church run by Polish missionaries: "When we arrived, I looked at the school across the street, and there were children, I don't know how many, forty, sixty, eighty children stacked up outside who had all been chopped up with machetes."[19] Dozens of other horrors unfolded over that hellish three-month period.

Tragically, not only did churches fail to provide a safe respite from the butchery, but in a number of cases Tutsis were actually *targeted* by church leaders. This brings us to the disturbing case of Elizaphan Ntakirutimana, a leader in the Seventh-day Adventist Church with impeccable theological and pastoral credentials. In the middle of the genocide several Tutsi Adventist pastors wrote Ntakirutimana a letter

---

18. Cited in Samantha Powers, *A Problem from Hell: America and the Age of Genocide* (New York: Harper Perennial, 2003), 381.

19. Cited in Powers, *A Problem from Hell*, 349.

appealing for help that opened with this haunting line: "We wish to inform you that tomorrow we will be killed with our families."[20] Instead of providing assistance to the Tutsis, Ntakirutimana directed Hutu militias to the Mugonero complex where they were hiding, resulting in a grisly slaughter. So in the cruelest irony the Christian these saints appealed to for salvation instead became their chief executioner. Although Ntakirutimana managed to avoid prosecution for several years, in 2003 he was finally convicted of the crime of genocide by the International Criminal Tribunal for Rwanda.

At the same time that a number of church leaders like Ntakirutimana either stood by or actively joined the genocide, a few brave souls struggled to save what lives they could. One of those was Mbaye Diagne, a captain from the Senegalese army—and a devout Muslim. Working for UN forces, Diagne repeatedly flouted the orders of his commanding officer to remain within the compound. Instead he ventured out time and again to pick up Tutsis in his Jeep—about five at a time—and transfer them to the relative safety of the compound. In order to accomplish this feat, he repeatedly bargained his way across dozens of Hutu checkpoints, using little more than cigarettes and his good humor. In this way, Diagne worked tirelessly for several weeks, repeatedly putting his life at risk until he was finally killed on May 31 from flying shrapnel.

Now for the application of the story. When I have asked Christians to choose whether belief or action takes priority in the Christian life, people typically respond that the question entails a false dichotomy. I am told that both are important, and so they cannot choose between them. While it is certainly true that both are important, the question does not depend on a false dilemma. We can illustrate the point as follows. Imagine that it is judgment day and that you are to appear before the throne of God. Further, you have the choice of which of

---

20. See Philip Gourevitch, *We Wish to Inform You That Tomorrow We Will Be Killed with Our Families* (New York: Farrar, Straus and Giroux, 1998).

these two lives you would prefer to have lived. Would you prefer to have lived the life of Elizaphan Ntakirutimana, a theologically orthodox participant in genocide? Or would you opt to be Mbaye Diagne, a Muslim who lost his life selflessly protecting the innocent in that genocide?[21] Let us be clear that this is not a false dichotomy: it is a real choice. So which will we choose?

Many Christians, liberals among them, have looked at Jesus' parable of the sheep and goats and have concluded that they would sooner side with the Muslim. Their reasoning is not that his works save him (for only Christ saves), but rather that his life is more likely to be a sign of a saving relationship with God. That is, true discipleship is more likely to be found in compelling moral action rather than in complicated doctrinal beliefs. New Testament scholar William Barclay makes the point when commenting on the parable of the Good Samaritan: "A heretic he [the Samaritan] may have been, but the love of God was in his heart. It is not uncommon to find the orthodox more interested in dogmas than in help and to find those the orthodox despise to be the ones who show the greatest love for others. *In the end we will be judged not by the creed we hold but by the life we lived.*"[22] In light of this kind of reflection many Christians, some self-described liberals as well as others like William Barclay, would find themselves siding with the inspiring legacy of Mbaye Diagne, despite his deeply mistaken theology. Put simply, they would sooner die affirming the wrong doctrines but acting rightly than affirming the right doctrines but acting wrongly. Even if you would prefer to have Ntakirutimana's legacy of orthodox belief and horrific practice, I hope

---

21. We could debate whether or not the notion of a Muslim being saved is more radical than the question of a Christian liberal being saved. But if it is, that actually works in the illustration's favor, for if we would sooner be the pious Muslim than the genocidal orthodox Christian, how much more yet would we prefer to be a pious Christian liberal than the genocidal orthodox Christian?

22. William Barclay, *The Gospel of Luke* (Louisville, KY: Westminster John Knox Press, 2001), 166, emphasis added.

you can appreciate why another Christian would opt for Diagne's legacy of aberrant belief and praiseworthy practice. And if we concede that much, then we must conclude that there is something to be said for a liberal view that the deepest roots of Christian identity are found in the soil of ethical action rather than doctrinal assent.

Coda

Let's go back to Ted and his rather testy attitude toward St. Joseph's Episcopal Church. What can we learn in this chapter about what might be the best way for him to interact with this church? To say the least, we can see that it is wrong to vilify certain people who are more liberal than we are in certain matters of doctrine and practice. Instead, we should strive to treat all with courtesy and charity and always to listen as well as argue. Many of us are eager to judge the liberals in our community, but might even the most rigorously orthodox of us have something to repent for? Dave Tomlinson raised this evocative possibility as follows:

> Jesus told a parable to a gathering of evangelical leaders. "An evangelical speaker and a liberal bishop each sat down to read the Bible. The evangelical speaker thanked God for the precious gift of the Holy Scriptures and pledged himself once again to proclaim them faithfully. 'Thank you God,' he prayed, 'that I am not like this poor bishop who doesn't believe your Word and seems unable to make his mind up whether or not Christ rose from the dead.' The bishop looked puzzled as he flicked through the pages of the Bible and said, 'Virgin birth, water into wine, physical resurrection. These things are hard to believe in Lord. In fact, I'm not even sure I'm in touch with you in a personal way. But I'm going to keep on searching.'
>
> "I tell you," said Jesus, "that this other man went home justified before God. For those who think they

have arrived have just barely started out, but those who continue searching are closer to the destination than they realize."[23]

---

23. Dave Tomlinson, *The Post-Evangelical*, rev. North American ed. (El Cajon, CA: emergentYS books; Grand Rapids, MI: 2003), 69–70.

8

NOT ALL
DARWINISTS
ARE MONKEYS

The documentary *Religulous* is not exactly highbrow entertainment.[1] For two hours the viewer is subjected to comedic atheist (or atheistic comedian) Bill Maher as he travels around the world, interviewing the religiously devout. The method of the film is straightforward: interview religious people; mock their ridiculous beliefs (with a kind of morbid fascination and a seemingly endless series of giggles); repeat. While many of Maher's exchanges with "true believers" are on the lighthearted (if sardonic) side, his interview with young-earth creationist Ken Ham takes on a more ominous tone. Ham is the president of Answers in Genesis, the leading young-earth creationist organization in the United States and the head of the Creation Museum of Petersburg, Kentucky. Given his prominence, millions of conservative evangelicals look to Ham and his organization for the ammunition to rebut evolutionists. During their increasingly tense conversation, Maher pointed out to Ham that where evolution is concerned, "Scientists line up overwhelmingly on one side of this issue. It would have to be an enormous conspiracy going on between scientists of all different disciplines in all different countries to have such a

---

1. The word "religulous" is a portmanteau of "religion" and "ridiculous."

consensus. That doesn't move you?" Ham was completely unfazed: "No, not at all, because from a biblical perspective I understand why the majority would not agree with the truth. Man is a sinner. Man is in rebellion against his Creator."

The statement is a striking one, for if Ham is to be believed, then the vast majority of scientists accept Darwinian evolution (that is, the theory that the diversity of species is explained through natural selection and random mutation) not because it provides the best explanation of the facts but rather because those very scientists are in sinful rebellion against God. Nor is Ham unique in making this charge. According to scientist and theologian Denis Lamoureux many antievolutionist Christians are convinced that scientists accept the theory for reasons ranging from gross incompetence to outright conspiracy: "Many Christians confidently claim that there is no scientific evidence to support human evolution. At best, they argue that the physical data is misinterpreted; at worst, they believe that it is fabricated and part of a secular conspiracy against Christianity." Lamoureux soberly added: "I once believed that the latter was the case."[2] And then there is Kent Hovind (aka Dr. Dino), who, prior to his 2006 arrest for tax evasion, was another very popular antievolutionist campaigner. The title of Hovind's booklet, *Are You Being Brainwashed? Propaganda in Science Textbooks*, says it all.[3] In the booklet Hovind asked, "Why would textbook authors teach lies just to get someone to believe in the theory of evolution? Why would anyone want to *brainwash* students into believing this theory?"[4] He then offered a number of reasons why scientists endorse evolution, ranging from gross incompetence (misinterpreting the facts) to deviousness (intentionally misrepresenting the

---

2. Denis Lamoureux, *I Love Jesus and I Accept Evolution* (Eugene, OR: Wipf and Stock, 2009), 124.

3. Hovind, *Are You Being Brainwashed? Propaganda in Science Textbooks* (Pensacola, FL: Creation Science Evangelism, 2007), 3.

4. Hovind, *Are You Being Brainwashed?* 25.

facts). While surface causes may differ, the bottom line is that "Satan is using lies to keep people from coming to Christ to be saved."[5] So Hovind agreed with Ham that the widespread acceptance of evolution within the scientific community can be traced to the Devil's influence.

A disturbing number of evangelicals believe that the widespread scientific consensus on evolution arises from a willful rebellion against God and his church. Not surprisingly, these same people tend to assume that evolution and Christianity are fundamentally at odds. (Presumably that is why the Devil is so keen to use it as a tool.) One of the most influential early statements of this basic incompatibility thesis came in 1874 when the great Princeton theologian Charles Hodge (then the premier defender of orthodoxy in North America) famously asked, "What is Darwinism?" and then provided his own sobering answer: "It is Atheism."[6] Many evangelicals today agree with Hodge's grim assessment. Consider Del Tackett's treatment of the topic in *The Truth Project* where he quoted the claim of atheist G. Richard Bozarth: "Evolution destroys utterly and finally the very reason Jesus' earthly life was supposedly made necessary. Destroy Adam and Eve and original sin, and in the rubble you will find the sorry remains of the Son of God . . . and if Jesus was not the redeemer who dies for our sins, and this is what evolution means, then Christianity is nothing" (session three).

If evolution really destroys the need for Jesus, it is hardly surprising that Christians will view it as the Devil's chosen tool for subverting the minds and souls of countless educated elites. This certainly explains Ted's virulent reaction to his young son Mark being wooed by Darwin's damnable theory. (Ted's horror could not have been much worse had the boy instead revealed that he was thinking of joining the Wiccan religion.)

---

5. Hovind, *Are You Being Brainwashed?* 25.

6. Charles Hodge, *What Is Darwinism?* (New York: Scribner, Armstrong, and Co., 1874), 177.

As widespread as these explanations are, when we think about it, the claim that people accept evolution because they are incompetent or wicked is pretty implausible. Surely, we would think, there must be at least *some* evidence that supports evolution. Yet critics like Ham and Hovind, and the millions of Christian conservatives who share their views, appear unwilling to concede even this. As Hovind said: "I am convinced that *all* of the 'evidences' that are currently being used to support the evolution theory are errors."[7] The unqualified nature of that statement is striking, particularly when we consider that the tens of thousands of highly educated scientists who accept evolution do not consider the theory to be of tangential importance. Rather, most agree (or at least are broadly sympathetic) with the title of the famous paper written by the great geneticist and Christian Theodosius Dobzhansky: "Nothing in Biology Makes Sense Except in the Light of Evolution."[8] When we contrast this widespread view with Hovind's striking claim that *evolution explains nothing*, it is not surprising that an individual must resort to the most sweeping charges of incompetence or conspiracy to explain why the theory is held so widely (and with such conviction) by educated elites.

Our primary concern in the chapter is not to consider whether evolution is true, but rather whether it is plausible to dismiss those who hold to it—many Christians included—as doing so out of incompetence, immorality, or both. In seeking an answer to this question, we will begin by considering the range of theological opinions shared by those who support Darwinian evolution. Next, we will consider if Darwinian evolution is really utterly baseless or whether it offers plausible explanations for at least some facts. Finally, we will consider whether there is a fundamental incompatibility between Darwinian

---

7. Hovind, *Are You Being Brainwashed?* 3, emphasis added.
8. *American Biology Teacher*, no. 35 (March 1973): 125–129. Even if the paper's title is hyperbolic, most scientists agree that Darwinian evolution is the cornerstone of contemporary biology.

evolution and Christianity by evaluating its implications for the image of God.

Listening to Evolutionary Biologists

As we have seen, the popular conservative Christian conception of the evolutionary scientist is pretty sobering: brainwashed and out to brainwash others through the popularization of a groundless theory that is utterly inimical to the gospel. In order to assess the plausibility of this claim we need to listen to evolutionary scientists themselves. Not surprisingly, when we do, we find that the picture is substantially more complex.

We can begin assessing scholarly attitudes toward Darwinian evolution and God by considering a 1998 survey by Edward J. Larson and Larry Witham.[9] Larson and Witham based their survey on the work of James H. Leuba, who surveyed scientists in 1914 on their belief in a God who answers prayer. After surveying the general population of scientists as well as elite scientists, Leuba discovered that 40 percent of the first group affirmed belief in a God who answered prayer, but that number dropped to one-third in the elite group. In Larson and Witham's survey the percentage of general scientists who affirm a God who answers prayer surprisingly remained at 40 percent. At the same time, the percentage of elite scientists who accept this concept of God had dropped to 10 percent. And the lowest percentage of belief among elite scientists was found in the biologists, with only 5 percent believing in an intervening God.

It should not surprise us that the results of Larson and Witham's survey have been interpreted by some as establishing the compatibility of evolution and Christian belief, while others have taken the opposite

---

9. Edward J. Larson and Larry Witham, "Scientists and Religion in America," *Scientific American* 281, no. 3 (1999): 88–93.

view.[10] Those who see compatibility point out that belief in God among general scientists has remained steady over several decades despite the widespread acceptance of evolutionary theory. Meanwhile, those who tout a basic incompatibility note that there has been a significant decrease of belief in God over the same period among elite scientists and particularly among evolutionary biologists. So which interpretation is right? One thing is clear: scientists themselves disagree over whether evolution and Christianity are incompatible.

Okay, so scientists clearly disagree over the religious implications of evolution. But what about the community of evangelical Christian scientists: Is there an antievolution consensus here? On the contrary, here too we find a diversity of opinion. While some evangelical scientists reject evolution completely, others throw their enthusiastic support behind the theory. The diversity is noted in a recent article in *Christianity Today* aptly titled "Darwin Divides."[11] The article focuses on a petition supporting new curriculum standards for Texas's students, which includes the statement that "evolution is an easily observable phenomenon that has been documented beyond any reasonable doubt." A number of the signatories were professors from Christian universities in Texas including Baylor, Hardin-Simmons, McMurry, and Texas Christian. One biology teacher from Abilene Christian University stated: "I hope to reach others on the weightier matters of the Resurrection, hope of eternal life, and the kingdom of heaven while I work out how evolution does not have to conflict with Christianity."[12] This individual is representative of many evangeli-

---

10. For a positive interpretation of the Larson-Witham survey for evolution and Christianity, see Denis Lamoureux, *Evolutionary Creation: A Christian Approach to Evolution* (Eugene, OR: Wipf and Stock, 2008), 6–7. For a negative interpretation, see Richard Dawkins, *The God Delusion* (Boston: Mariner, 2008), 126–127.

11. Bobby Ross Jr., "Darwin Divides," *Christianity Today* (online) at http://www.christianitytoday.com/ct/2009/april/1.18.html.

12. Cited in Ross, "Darwin Divides," http://www.christianitytoday.com/ct/2009/april/1.18.html.

cal Christians who are trained in the biological sciences and find no incompatibility with Darwin.

So what should we think about those Christians scientists who say, "I love Jesus and I accept evolution"?[13] For some Christians—particularly those who have long been exposed only to the work of nuts-and-bolts antievolution apologists like Ken Ham and Kent Hovind—it is a shock to discover the large and growing support for Darwin among people of faith. And yet this is not a new phenomenon. Indeed, since the time that Darwin published *The Origin of Species*, the theory of evolution has attracted enthusiastic supporters from the Christian, and specifically evangelical, community. For instance, Asa Gray, a contemporary of Darwin and America's leading botanist of the nineteenth century, played a crucial role in popularizing Darwinism in North America.[14] Nor was Gray's response particularly exceptional. James Moore, one of the leading Darwin historians, observed: "With but few exceptions the leading Christian thinkers in Great Britain and America came to terms quite readily with Darwinism and evolution."[15] Today there are many important Christian scientists who openly embrace evolution, perhaps the most well known being evangelical Francis Collins, the former head of the Human Genome Project.

A number of Christian theologians also accepted Darwin's theory early on, among them that early champion of fundamentalism James Orr as well as Charles Hodge's great successor at Princeton Seminary, B. B. Warfield. However, the real trend has come in the last few decades. Today the vast majority of Christian theologians writing in the area of science-theology relations accept evolution, including

13. See Lamoureux, *I Love Jesus and I Accept Evolution*.

14. See David N. Livingstone, *Darwin's Forgotten Defenders: The Encounter between Evangelical Theology and Evolutionary Thought* (Vancouver: Regent College Publishing, 1984).

15. *The Post-Darwinian Controversies: A Study of the Protestant Struggle to Come* (Cambridge: Cambridge University Press, 1981), 92.

Alister McGrath, John Polkinghorne, R. J. Russell, Ted Peters, Arthur Peacocke, Ian Barbour, Philip Clayton, Nancey Murphy, and many, many others. Does it not strain the limits of credulity to suggest that all these learned individuals, people who have spent their careers carefully reflecting on the relationship between science and Christianity, are either utterly incompetent or in service to the dark lord?

Does Darwinism Fit the Evidence?

Every fall, another group of young evangelicals leaves home, church, and family for the first time in order to study at a university. Once there, many of them engage in their first serious study of Darwinian evolution. While they may have heard much secondhand information about Darwin and his theory over the years at church and youth group, much of that information will be of questionable scientific accuracy.[16] Nonetheless, having been raised in this evangelical subculture, by the time they head off to a university, they will likely have formed strong convictions about the incompatibility of Darwinism and faith. In addition, many believe that Darwinism represents a collection of claims that are, if not demonstrably absurd and patently ridiculous, at least not supported by the evidence. And behind it all we find that deepest concern that evolution is ultimately a lie of the Enemy, propagated to attack the true faith.

What do you suppose happens when these students first discover that the Darwinian professors they study under week after week appear to be both highly intelligent and not particularly wicked? This was the very practical dilemma faced by Ted's son Mark, and it left

---

16. For instance, the common quip that evolution is "only a theory, not a fact" evinces a fundamental misunderstanding of the meaning of the term *theory*. Within science, a theory is a formal theoretical framework for interpreting facts as with the theory of gravity, the germ theory of disease, and the theory of plate tectonics. None of these explanatory frameworks is called a theory because it is not yet a "fact." Indeed, each one provides a satisfying explanation for many facts.

him with a crisis of authority: Would he continue to follow detractors from evolution that he met in Sunday school and youth group like Answers in Genesis president Ken Ham? Or would he be swayed by the testimony of brilliant evolutionary biologists like the 2006 Nobel laureate Craig Mello? Some students will side with the likes of Ham and, for better or worse, will suffer the social consequences from an educational system that is often intolerant of dissent. Others, like Mark, will take the path of least resistance, drawn by the "siren call" of evolution's dazzling intellectual firepower. Sadly, this course will often culminate in a heated debate with bewildered parents over turkey and dressing, and perhaps a deeper crisis of faith down the road.

So what should we think about this conflict of experts? At this point we can get some guidance in thinking through the pertinent issues by considering the argument from common consent. This argument, which used to be much more popular among Christian apologists than it is now, proceeds on the premise that it is most reasonable to believe that God exists in light of the overwhelming consensus of belief that God exists. While atheists have often sought to challenge the argument by pointing out that the majority can sometimes be wrong, or by maligning the argument as a mere appeal to authority, all things being equal it is surely the more rational course to follow a consensus. With that in mind, it is intriguing to note that the same principle could be applied to sway us on a scientific issue like Darwinism. When seeking to judge whether the theory has scientific merit, we should discern whether there is a scientific consensus among those informed of the relevant evidence. To be sure, there is some dissent over evolutionary theory, but then the consensus argument does not require *unanimous* consent, which is rarely if ever attained in science (or anywhere else for that matter). Rather, it seeks a substantial consensus, perhaps something north of 70 or 80 percent. If such a consensus exists among scientists concerning a particular theory, then it is reasonable for those of us unfamiliar with all the relevant data to side with the consensus that the theory is likely true. (And even if we don't go that far, it is at least reasonable to conclude that it is not necessarily a sign of foolishness or wickedness to follow such a consensus.)

So now the question: How can we discern whether a consensus exists in favor of Darwinism? On this point I propose that we begin on the negative side by considering a famous list compiled by the Discovery Institute (a conservative think tank in Seattle) called "Dissent from Darwinism." The list is significant because, as the title suggests, its purpose is to establish precisely that there is no scientific consensus on Darwin. By 2008 (the last time the list was updated) the list had grown to over 760 names, many of them scientists at leading universities around the world.[17] Based on the impressive "Dissent from Darwinism" list, we might conclude that there is sufficient intellectual weight behind the dissenters to back up the skepticism of critics like Ham and Hovind and throw significant doubt on Darwin's theory.

However, such a judgment is premature for it misses a crucial piece of data: How many scientists *accept* Darwinian evolution? Only when we have this number can we determine whether the seven-hundred-plus names collected on "Dissent from Darwinism" are substantial enough to undermine a significant consensus on the theory. With this in mind, a rather interesting alternative list was compiled by the National Center for Science Education (NCSE). Called "Project Steve" (in honor of famed paleontologist Stephen Jay Gould), the NCSE's list arbitrarily (and rather cheekily) limited signatories to scientists named Steve (as well as cognates like "Estevan"). Even with this very restrictive criterion in place, the Steve List had grown to include well over one thousand Steves by July 2009. In light of the estimate that about 1 percent of scientists have the name Steve,

---

17. The website for the list is found at http://www.dissentfromdarwin.org/. The entire list can be downloaded at http://www.discovery.org/scripts/viewDB/filesDB-download.php?command=download&id=660.

an unrestricted list in favor of Darwinism could presumably attract upward of 100,000 science professionals.[18] When juxtaposed against the "Dissent from Darwinism" list, this gives us an approximate figure that *less than 1 percent of scientists dissent from Darwinian evolutionary theory.* So despite the initial impression conveyed by the "Dissent from Darwinism" list, an overwhelming (if not universal) consensus still exists in favor of Darwinian evolution.

The detractor from our common consent argument could point out that it is *possible* that 99 percent of scientists could be completely wrong. True enough, but is it likely? And can sweeping appeals to gross ineptitude and sinful conspiracy really be used to dismiss such an impressive consensus? Again, please keep in mind that I am not arguing that the consensus is always right. Indeed, I am not even arguing that it is *probably* right since I am not seeking to mount a case for Darwinism per se. Rather my concern is simply to argue that it is implausible to explain the widespread support for evolution among scientists purely by way of incompetence and/or wickedness. As modest as this goal might be, the implications are striking. When Mark comes home for Thanksgiving and shares his new Darwinian convictions with his horrified father, it means that Ted should not treat Mark's professors—and the tens of thousands of scientists, professors, and Nobel laureates who stand with them—as if they were mere imbeciles or devious coconspirators. Instead, he should put down his drumstick, take a deep breath, and do his best to listen.

Once we have conceded that at least some of the consensus for Darwinian evolution is likely driven by the evidence, we should inquire into the nature of the evidence itself. Clearly it is far beyond the scope of the present work to consider the full extent of the evidence, ranging from anthropology to zoology, that is invoked in support of

---

18. See "Project Steve" at http://ncseweb.org/taking-action/project-steve.

evolution.[19] Instead, I will consider one particular line of evidence that has only emerged in the last few years. That fascinating line of evidence comes from the human genome and provides support for the Darwinian claim that human beings share common ancestry with the higher primates and in particular chimpanzees.

Though the morphological similarities between human beings and the higher primates are obvious, a fuller understanding of the genetic relationship has only begun to emerge in the last decade. Among the impressive discoveries is the fact that human beings share 97 percent of their genome with chimpanzees. While many Darwinians interpret this as offering support for common ancestry, genetics has also long provided a critical stumbling block to the thesis of common descent. The problem is that common descent requires that human beings have the same number of chromosomes as the great apes, but they do not: the great apes have twenty-four pairs of chromosomes, but human beings have only twenty-three. Left unchallenged, this fact alone would be sufficient to undermine the common descent hypothesis (at least with respect to humans and the great apes). The nature of the problem can be explained with the following analogy. Let's say that Archie is initially implicated in the murder of Jughead based on the eyewitness testimony of Veronica. Even if this is all the prosecutor had, it might be enough to convict Archie. However when Dilton subsequently discovers Reggie's DNA on the murder weapon, this is sufficient to show that Veronica must be wrong: Archie is not guilty; Reggie is. Similarly, while the initial case for human beings sharing common descent with chimpanzees (evidence that includes similar morphology, 97 percent shared DNA, and a shared vitamin C deficiency) might appear strong, the discovery of contrasting numbers of

19. See, for instance, Jerry A. Coyne, *Why Evolution Is True* (New York: Viking, 2009); Kenneth Miller, *Only a Theory: Evolution and the Battle for America's Soul* (New York: Penguin, 2009); Richard Dawkins, *The Greatest Show on Earth: The Evidence for Evolution* (New York: Free Press, 2009).

chromosomes is so significant that it is sufficient to undermine the common descent hypothesis as surely as new DNA evidence would undermine the case against Archie.

There is one way to reconcile the contrasting numbers of chromosomal pairs between humans and chimps with the thesis of common descent, and that is if one pair of human chromosomes fused at some past point in our evolutionary history. Since this provided a testable prediction, scientists set about to discover whether the human genome contained the expected fused chromosomal pair. And sure enough, just as the Darwinian hypothesis of common descent had predicted, a fused pair was indeed discovered in the human genome at chromosome 2.[20]

So how have Darwin dissenters responded to this discovery? Consider the response of two well-known critics of Darwinism: Casey Luskin and Logan Paul Gage. Luskin and Gage concede that chromosome 2 is fused, but they reject the inference that this discovery supports common ancestry: "Evidence for chromosomal fusion in humans simply indicates that, at some point within our human lineages, two chromosomes became fused. This tells us nothing about whether we share a common ancestor with apes."[21] Technically speaking they are correct: the discovery of a fused chromosome does not necessitate the conclusion that humans share common ancestry with the higher primates. But even so, surely this discovery yields at least *some* evidential credibility to the common descent hypothesis. To illustrate the reasoning here, consider the following analogy. A child

---

20. See "Initial Sequence of the Chimpanzee Genome and Comparison with the Human Genome," *Nature*, vol. 437 (2005): 69–87. For an accessible discussion of the evidence, see Francis Collins, *The Language of God: A Scientist Presents Evidence for Belief* (New York: Free Press, 2007), 137–141.

21. Casey Luskin and Logan Paul Gage, "A Reply to Francis Collins's Darwinian Arguments for Common Ancestry of Apes and Humans," in *Intelligent Design 101: Leading Experts Explain the Key Issues*, ed. H. Wayne House (Grand Rapids, MI: Eerdmans, 2008), 220.

comes to school and tells his teacher that his dog ate his homework. While the teacher is understandably skeptical of this well-worn alibi, she is nonetheless sufficiently open minded to entertain it, but *only* if the student can provide corroborating evidence. And so the teacher replies: "If the dog really did eat your homework, then evidence of it should turn up in its feces. So we'll just wait and see." And with that the two sit down to keep vigil until the dog has its bowel movement. Finally, after several hours the dog does its business and, lo and behold, bits of paper are visible in the feces. In other words, the evidence that was predicted by the claim has now been verified. Of course, the teacher could now reply that the evidence is inadequate to validate the alibi because the paper could have come from another source. But this response would surely strike us as special pleading. At the very least, the discovery of the paper would have greatly increased the plausibility of the student's "dog ate my homework" alibi since a testable prediction has been vindicated. By the same token, the discovery of a fused chromosome greatly increases the plausibility of the common descent hypothesis.

Before leaving this section behind, we should reiterate one more time the terribly modest goal of the argument. I am not arguing that evolution is true or even likely true. All I have been concerned to argue in this section is that there is an impressive consensus among scientists across a broad range of fields from anthropology to zoology that evolution is true and that it is most reasonable to conclude that this consensus has been generated, at least in part, because of the explanatory power of Darwinian evolutionary theory. As a result, we ought to reject the attempt to dismiss this broad consensus by suggesting that it arises from incompetence and/or immorality. Instead we ought to consider that evidence openly and honestly.

Is Darwinism Compatible with the Image of God?

Gather together as much evidence in favor of evolution as you like, and some people will still reject it without a second thought, for they are utterly *convinced* that evolution *must* be false. One reason for this certainty comes back to Hodge's conviction that Darwinism is atheism, and if not quite atheism, then something in the neighborhood. This is the way Henry Morris put it: "One can be a Christian and an evolutionist, just as one can be a Christian thief, or a Christian adulterer, or a Christian liar. It is absolutely impossible for those who profess to believe the Bible and to follow Christ to embrace evolutionism."[22] Boiled down to essentials, the argument goes something like this:

1. I am certain that Christianity is true.

2. If Christianity is true, then Darwinism is false.

3. Therefore, Darwinism is false.

It is hardly surprising that people motivated by this type of reasoning are no more likely to consider evolution seriously than they are likely to consider polygamy, murder, or Wicca. But is the reasoning itself sound?

For many evangelicals, confirmation of their antagonism toward evolution came in the 2008 pro-intelligent design documentary *Expelled: No Intelligence Allowed* (a film that Ted first saw on the big screen at his church). In the film comedian Ben Stein determined to investigate the alleged marginalization of intelligent design by the scientific establishment. While concerns of academic freedom and censorship are prevalent in the film, we do not need to probe far beneath the surface to find the smoldering sentiment that Darwinian evolution is fundamentally incompatible with Christian convictions.

---

22. Henry Morris cited in R. J. Berry, *God and Evolution: Creation, Evolution, and the Bible* (Vancouver: Regent College Publishing, 2000), 13.

To this end, Stein interviewed a number of atheists in the film who claimed that Darwin is irreconcilable with faith. For instance, atheist Will Provine declared: "No god, no life after death, no ultimate foundation for ethics, no ultimate meaning in life, and no human free will are all deeply connected to an evolutionary perspective. You're here today and you're gone tomorrow and that's all there is to it." If Provine is correct, evolution contradicts a number of essential Christian doctrines. This certainly is a startling claim, but rather than assess it critically, Stein simply accepted it with the observation that "Dr. Provine's deconversion story was typical amongst the Darwinists we interviewed." The point is further hammered home when Stein interviewed atheists Richard Dawkins and P. Z. Myers, who are also well known for their unremitting hostility toward religion. And so Stein concluded, "It appears Darwinism does lead to atheism." Hodge, it would seem, is vindicated.

While the perspective of Provine, Dawkins, and Myers deserves to be heard, we might wonder why Stein didn't interview any of the thousands of Christian theologians and scientists who are Darwinians. In fact he did. He just didn't let the viewers know about it. In the film Stein interviewed two theistic evolutionists, Alister McGrath and John Polkinghorne, both respected theologians with extensive training in science (indeed, Polkinghorne was once a theoretical physicist). Sadly enough, while Stein invited McGrath and Polkinghorne to share their views on the compatibility of Christianity and science, he never invited them to share their perspective on the compatibility of Christianity and Darwinian evolution. Stein also interviewed Eugenie Scott, the executive director for the National Center for Science Education. While Scott is an atheist, she did not agree with Provine, Dawkins, and Myers that Christianity and evolution are incompatible. Indeed, she observed that "the most important group we work with is members of the faith community because the best kept secret in this controversy is that Catholics and mainstream Protestants are okay on evolution." Clearly Stein was not happy with Scott's claim, and so her comment was immediately followed by journalist Larry Witham's incendiary rejoinder that Christian evolutionists are "liberals" who side with Darwin simply because of their deep antipathy toward religious conservatives. When he made this startling claim, Witham added another charge to explain why some assent to Darwinism: irascibility. That is, they opt for evolution because they just trying to stir up trouble among the faithful, rather like soccer hoodlums pouring out of an English pub in search of a good brawl.

But this additional option hardly helps us dismiss the carefully reasoned scientific and theological support for Darwin's theory offered by thoughtful scientist-theologians like McGrath and Polkinghorne. Witham followed his implausible irascibility charge by affirming Provine's claim that Darwinism and atheism are linked: "Implicit in most evolutionary theory is that either there is no god or god cannot have anything, any role in it. So naturally, as many evolutionists will say, it's the strongest engine for atheism." It may well be that some Christians are attracted to Darwin because of their antagonism toward conservative Christianity. But can that plausibly explain the temperate and well-articulated position taken by McGrath, Polkinghorne, and tens of thousands of other Christians?

As I said at the beginning of this section, some Christians are apparently moved to adopt sweeping condemnations of evolution (and its sympathizers) based on the assumption that it is simply incompatible with Christian faith. In addition, it also seems to be assumed that acceptance of Darwinian evolution will lead to great evil and suffering. For evidence of this we need only observe that many dissenters from Darwin have linked the theory with the horrors of Nazi Germany, and there is no more rhetorically effective charge than this.[23] This shocking link should give us a sense of the seriousness with which many view the rise of Darwinian evolution. To get a sense of the

---

23. See my article "It's Just Like Nazi Germany . . ." at http://www.christianpost.com/blogs/tentativeapologist/2009/09/its-just-like-nazi-germany-30/index.html.

urgency, put yourself back into Germany in the 1930s for a moment. Imagine that you are a witness to the rise of the Third Reich. Although many of your Christian friends are enthusiastic about Hitler, you are convinced that his political ideology will lead to the proliferation of evils like fascism, Neo-Paganism, and anti-Semitism. Once you have drawn these conclusions, the fact that a pro-Nazi consensus emerges in the German Lutheran Church would carry no persuasive force for you whatsoever. Indeed, you would be insulted by a friend who would attempt to persuade you to join the Nazis by appealing to a long list of pro-Nazi theologians and church leaders. Consequently, you would not shy away from dismissing all those in this pro-Nazi consensus list as being either ignorant of Nazism's true nature or as culpable supporters of a truly demonic regime.

Against that extreme backdrop, imagine a 1930s Bill Maher interviewing a Nazi-fighting Ken Ham. Nazi Maher points out that "scientists line up overwhelmingly on the pro-Hitler side of this issue. It would have to be an enormous conspiracy going on between scientists of all different disciplines to have such a consensus. That doesn't move you?" To this, Nazi-fighting Ham offers his resolute reply: "No, not at all, because from a biblical perspective I understand why the majority would not agree with the truth. Man is a sinner. Man is in rebellion against his Creator." While Ham's sweeping dismissal of current scientific consensus is indefensible, when we place it against the backdrop of a fear tantamount to Nazism, it becomes understandable, even admirable. We should keep this in mind when we countenance the overwhelming support that apologists like Ham receive from many in the mainstream conservative Christian population.

But even if that is the way crusaders like Ham are often perceived by their devotees, it merely begs the question of whether there are good reasons to believe that the theory of evolution will lead to evils akin to those committed by the Third Reich. Could it really be, as *Expelled* implies, that Darwinism clears the way for horrifying ideologies like Nazism? Obviously Darwinism is not anti-Semitic per se. So insofar as we see a link, it would arise from the perception that Darwinian evolution undermines human dignity generally, thereby clearing the way for abuses of human dignity like anti-Semitism. The concern is summarized in the title of Moody Adams's little booklet *Don't Let the Evolutionist Make a Monkey out of You.*[24] This title implies that Darwinian evolution is stupid since to make a monkey out of someone is to show them to be stupid or gullible, in this case by convincing them that something absurd is true. (The guy who convinced you that you could become a millionaire by investing five hundred bucks in his pyramid scheme made a monkey out of you. The Darwinist who aims to convince you that you're descended from monkeys is angling to do the same.) The title also has another, more somber, implication: Darwinian evolution undermines human value or dignity.[25] In this sense the Darwinist makes us into monkeys by undermining human worth. In other words, if we are merely animals, then we might as well live like animals.

But how does Darwinian evolution undermine human value exactly? Presumably the core problem is that of humble origins: once we accept that human beings share common ancestry with chimps (and indeed with the sea cucumbers at the city aquarium and even the algae growing in that kiddie pool sitting in your neighbor's backyard), it is impossible to retain any notion of our unique dignity and value. Perhaps we might illustrate the problem by considering the sobering story of the Cadillac Cimarron. Back in the early 1980s Cadillac decided to develop an entry-level automobile to introduce people to

---

24. (Baton Rouge, LA: Moody Adams Evangelistic Association, 1981).

25. This rhetorical tactic has been around for a while. As historian Michael Lienesch observed of the fundamentalist controversies in the 1920s, "Debates on evolution were littered with satiric references to 'monkey business,' 'monkeyshines,' 'monkeyfoolery,' and the like. But while both sides made use of such phrases, antievolutionists used them more easily and effectively, particularly in casting derision at the alleged biological relationship between monkeys and humans." *In the Beginning: Fundamentalism, the Scopes Trial, and the Making of the Antievolution Movement* (Chapel Hill, NC: University of North Carolina Press, 2007), 100.

the marque, the idea being that after a good experience with the car, these customers would trade up to a higher-priced model. Based on that reasoning the Cadillac Cimarron was unveiled in 1982—to an appalled public. The central problem was that Cadillac decided to develop the Cimarron on the cheap by basing the car on the Chevy Cavalier, a vehicle so bland that it would have blended right in on a communist-era East German car lot. In retrospect, the whole project was doomed from the start, for no serious, brand-conscious Cadillac consumer would ever buy a rebadged and overpriced Cavalier. Once the Cimarron's humble origins were known, its fate was effectively sealed.

According to the argument, the same problem of humble origins that sealed the fate of the Cadillac Cimarron besets the human being who is revealed to have a humble origin. If we conclude that we share common ancestry with nit-picking monkeys (let alone freaky sea cucumbers and scummy algae), we lose our special worth as surely as the much-loathed Cimarron. At best we are—as Desmond Morris infamously titled his book—*The Naked Ape*;[26] at worst we are little more than overpriced bags of oxygen, carbon, hydrogen, and nitrogen. As for "image of God," you might as well put a Gucci label on a garbage bag. Not surprisingly, severe consequences follow, for once human beings lose their intrinsic worth, the way is open for the descent into genocidal mutinies and other untold horrors: Hitler, here we come.

Sounds extreme you say? Well, consider that the London Zoo gained headlines in the summer of 2005 when it unveiled a display featuring eight human beings living "in their natural habitat" (though mercifully not "au naturel"—they were sporting swimsuits with pinned-on fig leaves). The people were free to walk around the enclosure, sun themselves on the rocks, and wave to passersby.

---

26. (New York: McGraw-Hill, 1967).

The sign on the enclosure identified the strange creatures as Homo sapiens, and it went on to describe their natural habitat and diet. The zoo spokeswoman explained the subversive point of the display as follows: "Seeing people in a different environment, among other animals . . . teaches members of the public that the human is *just another primate*."[27] It is that "just" that is so worrisome: *just* another primate; *just* another biped; *just* another mammal; *just another creature*. And once you have dehumanized humanity, we have set the conditions to treat human beings as objects. This in turn clears the way for the resurgence of demonic ideologies like Nazism. And if Darwinian evolution makes smooth the road to Nazism, we ought to fight it with unqualified vigor, even if that means dismissing Darwin's many supporters as either hopelessly uninformed baboons or the Devil's henchmen.

I agree that we ought to be extremely careful about any scientific theory that seems to undermine human dignity and thereby make possible the rise of militaristic and genocidal ideologies. But does evolution really do this? That is, does the claim that human beings share common ancestry with monkeys, sea cucumbers, and even lowly algae lead to a fatal denigration of human value? Frankly, I find this charge to be puzzling. After all, each one of us came from a sperm and an egg; neither of which is of much value in itself. Nobody laments the egg lost at every menstrual cycle, let alone the millions of sperm doomed to perish with each coital act. And yet, despite the terribly low status of egg and sperm, nobody worries that our humble origins in the union of the two somehow denigrates human value. Why? Surely the answer is obvious: however lowly our origins, *we* are not mere ova or sperm. Nobody would argue that because we come from the union of sperm and egg, we are nothing but glorified sperm and

---

27. Cited in Kevin Kechtkopf, "Humans on Display at London's Zoo," (August 26, 2005), CBS News online at http://www.cbsnews.com/stories/2005/08/26/world/main798423.shtml, emphasis added.

egg. But then why think that if we come from an evolutionary process from primitive single-cell organisms that we are therefore nothing but glorified primitive single-cell organisms? Surely our extraordinary achievements provide ample empirical evidence of humanity's unique status. Just consider the sonnets of Shakespeare, the art of Angelico, and the physics of Feynman (not to mention the ganache cake of celebrity chef Ina Garten).

Is it possible to get beyond the visceral "yuck factor" of thinking of chimps and algae as distant cousins? Can we find a more robust argument to demonstrate how common ancestry might be incompatible with human uniqueness? In order to answer that question, we should begin by identifying that set of qualities that is seen to distinguish human beings as having unique dignity and worth. Within biblical theology that unique status is commonly identified as the image (and likeness) of God. So the humble origins objection really amounts to this: the notion of human beings sharing common ancestry with other life-forms is incompatible with at least some of the unique characteristics of the image of God. Just as being married is incompatible with the concept bachelor, so the claim goes, sharing common ancestry is incompatible with the concept of the image of God.

Now here lies the difficulty. While the contradictory nature of a married bachelor is clear enough given the lucidity of the concept of bachelor, the concept of "commonly descended divine image bearer" does not likewise seem obviously contradictory. This is hardly surprising given that there is so much controversy on what the image of God even is. In Scripture we have only a smattering of texts that refer to the image or likeness of God (Genesis 1:26–27; 5:1; 9:6; 1 Corinthians 11:7; 15:49; James 3:9). What is striking about these texts is that they provide no clear picture of what the image (that is, the essence of human uniqueness) consists. As a result, there is no reason to believe that common ancestry is incompatible with the image. These texts simply do not provide sufficient grounds to conclude with confidence that a creature made in the image of God could not share common descent with other creatures that do not.[28]

One final point is worth mentioning. Even if there was evidence that image and/or likeness of God was somehow incompatible with common descent, we could still countenance the possibility of evolution, while adding that God intervened in the evolutionary process (perhaps uniquely at the creation of Adam) in such a way that he brought human beings a quantum leap beyond our nearest ancestors so that we could be divine image bearers. When we consider this additional possibility, I simply find no evidence to think that Darwinism necessarily undermines human dignity. And that means that I find no ground to justify the sweeping dismissal of the Darwinist in a way parallel to the sweeping dismissal of a Nazi sympathizer.[29]

Much remains to be said of course. One remaining elephant in the room concerns the way to interpret Genesis 1–3. Is it to be read as a straightforward historical narrative, as so many Christians assume? Here I will simply observe that many Old Testament scholars believe that Genesis 1–3 is not a historical narrative with scientific implications and thus that there is no conflict between this ancient text and contemporary Darwinism.[30] Here again my point is not that this type of nonhistorical reading is necessarily the best one. Rather, it is simply that many Christians adopt such a reading of Genesis with knowledge of the text and without any wicked intentions.

---

28. There are three main types of theories on the image of God: substantive, functional, and relational. I do not see how any of these theories support the intrinsic incompatibility between the image of God and common descent.

29. Interestingly, respected historians Adrian Desmond and James Moore argue that one reason Darwin set forth his evolutionary views was moral: he saw common ancestry as the basis to argue for abolition of slavery. See *Darwin's Sacred Cause: How a Hatred of Slavery Shaped Darwin's Views on Human Evolution* (New York: Houghton Mifflin Harcourt, 2009).

30. See Lamoureux, *Evolutionary Creation*, chapters 4–7.

Coda

Let's return to the practical realities of Christian parenting. But at this point we will switch from Ted and his son Mark to you. Your daughter Maggie has just graduated from her Christian high school and has been accepted at a leading university in the fall to study biology. To this point in her life Maggie has been taught that evolution is at best an erroneous theory utterly lacking in evidence and at worst a malicious attempt by the Enemy to subvert human dignity and the Christian gospel. You know that within months she will be sitting under the tutelage of leading intellectuals, including one who is a winner of the International Prize for Biology, another who is a Nobel laureate, and the whole lot of them convinced that Darwinian evolutionary theory is the unifying framework of contemporary biology. Do you spend your last few months with your daughter intently reinforcing hardened categories forged by the likes of Ham and Hovind in a last-ditch attempt to ensure that she continues to believe all evolutionists are hopeless ideologues marred by ignorance and corrupted by hostility to the true faith? Or do you use that time to cultivate in her an open attitude regarding the scientific evidence, a greater openness concerning the bounds of legitimate theological inquiry, and the recognition that the Bible just might be open to different readings? The choice is yours.

9

NOT ALL
ANIMAL RIGHTS
ACTIVISTS
ARE WACKOS

The interview started out much like any other: it was a pleasant June day in Washington, and President Barack Obama had just sat down with CNBC, a US television news and business channel. But this interview was different, very different. And it all came down to the presence of one very persistent and very obnoxious fly. After being repeatedly interrupted, President Obama finally reached the threshold of his patience. He paused, turned his attention fully toward the fly, and with a single deft swat of the hand he took the unsuspecting insect's life. Initially the press picked up the story as a humorous revelation of the president's excellent reflexes and, killer instincts. Of course, it was all in good humor, that is, until the animal rights group PETA (People for the Ethical Treatment of Animals) entered into the debate, apparently unaware that it was all a joke. Instead they mounted their soapbox by denouncing Obama's action in a press release as a callous "execution." PETA spokesman Bruce Friedrich pleaded with the president: "We believe that people, where they can be compassionate, should be, for all animals."[1] Even for flies apparently. And in a move to underline the message, PETA promptly sent the president a humane catch-and-release fly trap in the hopes of preventing the carnage of that dark day from ever being repeated.

The "Obama fly homicide" fiasco captures the familiar absurd side of animal rights activism. But there are at least two other faces that add a more somber note to evangelical perceptions: the obnoxious and the dangerous. The obnoxious image brings us to Ingrid Newkirk, the charismatic founder of PETA, which is the largest and most powerful animal rights organization in the world. According to her critics Newkirk has honed obnoxiousness to a fine art. Consider the scene in the documentary *I Am an Animal: The Story of Ingrid Newkirk and PETA*, which begins with Newkirk and a few coconspirators wearing heavy fur coats and lingering suspiciously outside the Jean Paul Gaultier Boutique in Paris. Suddenly they walk into the shop, past the clueless security guard, and straight into the display window. Within moments they are splattering the windows with blood-red paint and slapping up posters of dead skinned animals with the gripping byline "Death for Sale." It is easy to feel sympathy for the well-groomed and clearly dazed employees who are the hapless victims of this blitzkrieg protest.

If animal rights activism often appears to be ridiculous and obnoxious, it can also look downright dangerous. Here you might think of radical terrorist groups like the Animal Liberation Front (ALF), which is infamous for engaging in actions like breaking into research facilities to free lab animals. But such actions are relatively isolated actions undertaken by a few radicals. The real concern about the danger posed by animal rights extends far beyond isolated instances of civil disobedience down to the underlying general demotion of human beings to being just another animal, a premise captured in the title to the

---

1. See "PETA Miffed at President Obama's Fly 'Execution,'" at http://www.reuters.com/article/newsOne/idUSTRE55H4Z220090618.

above-mentioned documentary: *I Am an Animal*. PETA's demotion of human beings was on shocking display in its highly controversial 2003 Holocaust on Your Plate exhibition. The exhibition consisted of eight large panels that juxtaposed pictures of factory-farmed animals with images of the Holocaust, including a haunting image of Jewish men sandwiched into tiny bunks in a barracks alongside the image of chickens stacked in their battery cages. Equally shocking was the text that went with the images. Here's an excerpt: "Like the Jews murdered in concentration camps, animals are terrorized when they are housed in huge filthy warehouses and rounded up for shipment to slaughter. The leather sofa and handbag are the *moral equivalent* of the lampshades made from the skins of people killed in the death camps."[2]

Moral equivalent? Surely they cannot be serious. Or so we may want to tell ourselves. On the contrary, you can be sure that every image and sentence in this exhibition was carefully and purposefully chosen to ensure maximal emotional impact. Needless to say, the cumulative impact of Holocaust on Your Plate seems to be more concerned with demoting human value than elevating animals. Fly executions aside, it would seem that animal rights really is no laughing matter.

Not surprisingly, Ted holds these common perceptions that the animal rights movement is absurd, obnoxious, and dangerous, and that about summarizes his perspective on his animal rights neighbors as well. However, Ted will quickly add that even though he dislikes (more correctly, *despises*) the animal rights movement, this should not be interpreted as dislike for animals. Though Ted is a big meat eater, he still loves animals. Just consider his faithful companion Scraps, a mongrel that the family adopted some years ago from the local humane society. Or you could look to Ted's lifelong love of bird watching or to his defense of the local state park against encroaching development.

---

2. Cited in Wesley J. Smith, "PETA to Cannibals: Don't Let Them Eat Steak,"
San Francisco Chronicle (Dec. 21, 2003), emphasis added. Cited at http://www.sfgate.
com/cgi-bin/article.cgi?file=/chronicle/archive/2003/12/21/INGH63PBJ81.DTL.

But while Ted views himself as an animal lover, he still perceives animal rights activists to be ridiculous, obnoxious, and dangerous. And all this colors Ted's perspective as he stares back across the fence at his wacky animal rights neighbors with their moral superiority, proudly sitting astride a topsy-turvy set of values.

If Ted is a reliable barometer of evangelicals, animal rights activists have their work cut out for them, certainly if they hope to garner some sympathy for their cause. But we will not limit ourselves here to popular perceptions. Instead we will seek to understand what motivates animal rights activists at their core and what we as Christians can learn from them. I will argue that when we push beyond the more sensational cases beloved of the media we will find at the core of animal rights not a desire to demote human beings but rather an admirable concern to alleviate unnecessary animal suffering. And while we may never all agree on the exact moral status of animals and the full range of our obligations toward them, I think we can go far to appreciating the animal rights call for a deepened moral consistency and moral compassion for all sentient life. Indeed, I will argue in our final section that based on such newfound sympathies we might even begin to read Scripture in a new, more animal-friendly light.

What Motivates Animal Rights Activism?

Many evangelicals like Ted largely derive their perception of animal rights as absurd, obnoxious, and dangerous from media reports like Obama's fly swatting and the infamous Holocaust on Your Plate exhibition. This tide of negative press is complemented by the unsympathetic analysis of the movement from many conservative Christian leaders. We find a typical example in Chuck Colson's brief 2003 essay (delivered on his *Breakpoint* radio program) titled "Happy Cows,

Unhappy People."[3] Colson began by criticizing PETA and other animal rights groups for focusing on trivial cases of animal advocacy. After noting some absurd examples (reminiscent of the Obama fly execution), Colson commented: "You have to laugh at stories like these." But Colson quickly moved from the absurd to the dangerous as he next drew attention to the misanthropic tendency of animal rights. He warned that the animal rights movement depends on "speciesism," the doctrine that human beings are morally equivalent to other creatures such that any attempt to assert our superiority is as arbitrary and immoral as racism (hence, *species*-ism). And we need look no further for corroboration than the statements of animal rights activists themselves. Indeed, Newkirk infamously declared: "There is no rational basis for separating out the human animal. A rat is a pig is a dog is a boy. They're all animals."[4] Colson asserted that speciesism (and presumably animal rights) "challenges Christianity's most fundamental doctrines." Next he noted that "ominously some animal rights activists carry their logic to extremes: that if it's 'murder' to kill chicken, for instance, it's morally acceptable to stop the 'murderer.'" So, Colson saw the extension to violence against human beings to be a natural next step. [5]

If evangelical critics like Colson are adamant that animal rights is immoral, other critics focus on the sheer idiocy of the animal rights cause. For an excellent (and entertaining) example we need look no further than the Vegetable Rights Militant Movement website, which provides a clever parody of animal rights. On the website (found

---

3. Colson, "Happy Cows, Unhappy People: The Rise of Animal 'Rights,'" (Jan. 28, 2003), http://www.breakpoint.org/commentaries/2926-happy-cows-unhappy-people.

4. Cited in Stephen Garrard Post, *Inquiries in Bioethics* (Washington, DC: Georgetown University Press, 1993), 162.

5. Of course most social and political movements attract some fringe extremists who are willing to resort to violence to further the cause. For instance, some in the pro-life movement have killed abortion doctors and bombed clinics. But then if every group attracts extremists, why pick on animal rights activists?

at vegetablecruelty.com) we read: "The Vegetable Rights Militant Movement (VRMM) is a nationally active, grassroots, vegetable liberation and defense organization. The VRMM differs from other vegetable activist organizations in that it really does all that it can to stop people from torturing, killing, humiliating, and ultimately eating vegetables and fruits."

Perhaps the most effective section of the website is the "Gallery of Atrocities," which contains a number of highly "disturbing" pictures of fruit and vegetables being shipped to market in terribly cramped conditions and being callously sliced open with knives. Try to imagine carrots being chopped up *right in front of you*, and you get a sense of the horror. But even if the website is good for a laugh at the expense of animal lovers, we need to ask whether the concerns of animal rights activists really are as idiotic as vegetablecruelty.com would have us believe. Is it really as absurd to fight to liberate chickens from battery cages as it would be to "free" bananas from crates? And what about Colson's sober assessment? Is animal rights activism really this immoral and dangerous? Is the plea for animal rights really, at its core, a fundamental assault on *human* dignity?

As in our other cases, the first step to answering these questions is found in listening. To do that let's return to the documentary *I Am an Animal*. The film opens with Newkirk reading aloud some of the hate mail she receives on a daily basis. (To give you a sense of the volatility, one of the less vulgar letters expresses the hope that Newkirk will someday be killed and eaten by a serial killer.) As we listen to Newkirk stoically read these letters, we are confronted with the utter hatred that is often directed against the animal rights movement, much of it from self-described Christians. However, while we might not agree with the sentiments, is some sort of hostility not to be expected? After all, animal rights activists hate human beings, don't they? Perhaps *some* would qualify as misanthropes, but this certainly isn't the impression that comes out of the interview with Newkirk (or with other leading animal rights defenders like Tom Regan, Peter Singer, and Gary

Francione). Newkirk does not seem particularly interested in demoting human beings. Rather, her passion and mission is simply to get people to stop inflicting suffering on animals: "For my whole adult life I have felt absolutely driven to try to convince people to consider animals no matter what they're doing: whether they're buying something to eat or whether they've got a dog in their house. They've got to think of what that animal is going through and to put that animal in the equation."[6] Note that when it comes to her core, driving concern, there is no mention of speciesism. Rather, there is only a call to human beings to reflect morally on the fact that animals are sentient creatures that suffer tremendously as a result of our callousness and insensitivity. To drive the point home, Newkirk recounted the following story from her youth in India when she witnessed a bull being abused:

> I looked out—you could see the street from my dining room—and a man was beating this, um, this bull came along pulling a cart, and he obviously was having trouble and as I watched the man started to really beat him. And then he lifted the bull's tail and he put the stick up into his rectum. And this bull screamed and then he collapsed. And the man raised his stick and started to . . . And I dropped my soup spoon and ran out into the street. And I was just filled with so much anger and panic to stop this from happening to this being. And I got there and I tore the stick away from him—I was only about eight and a half probably—and I made him kneel down just filled with rage.[7]

After watching *I Am an Animal*, it is clear that the deepest roots of Newkirk's ethical stance are not found in the soil of misanthropy. Rather, she seemed (to me at least) to be focused on raising the profile

---

6. *I Am an Animal: The Story of Ingrid Newkirk and PETA.*
7. *I Am an Animal: The Story of Ingrid Newkirk and PETA.*

of animals under duress so as to reduce their suffering, even if it sometimes means cheap publicity grabs like the ridiculous Obama fly fiasco. Newkirk surely cannot be dismissed as uninformed about the issues, for she has probably thought much more consistently about animal suffering than the vast majority of Christians who have never given their ham sandwich a second thought. We may disagree with Newkirk's conviction that animal suffering ought to weigh equally in our judgments as concern for human suffering. But can we not at least agree with her that unnecessary animal suffering is an evil that we ought to strive to eliminate? Surely Christians can share Newkirk's outrage at the abominable treatment of that bull. But if we can do this, then surely we can share Newkirk's concern for the thousands of animals that are trampled without a second thought every day. Indeed, Christians should have additional motives here. For one thing, we believe humans are called by God to be responsible stewards of creation (Genesis 1:28), and that mandate includes the flourishing of animals. Moreover, we believe that the world is governed by a God who watches over the fall of the sparrow as surely as the cycling of the heavens.

I certainly agree that calling the killing of a fly an "execution" is absurd. But then many animal rights activists would agree. Indeed, they would consider PETA's press release on the incident to constitute a trite and counterproductive publicity grab. They recognize as well as most of us that such outrageous statements only serve to marginalize the more serious aspects of the animal rights movement. We should no more assume that PETA or any other animal rights organization (or individual) represents the movement than that animal rights activists should assume that one particular evangelical organization or individual represents the evangelical community. So the next time you are tempted to dismiss animal rights because PETA issued a ridiculous statement or the ALF (Animal Liberation Front) engaged in an act of terrorism, remember how you would feel about evangelicals being similarly dismissed because of the actions of a few.

Colson ended his article with a nod toward animals: "As Christians, we have a moral duty to respect the animal world as God's handiwork, treating animals with 'the mercy of our Maker.'" If evangelicals really took this statement seriously and thought through its full moral implications, I suspect that much of the tension with animal rights would disappear. If Newkirk's sentiments are indicative of the moral heart of many animal rights activists (as they undoubtedly are), then there may be substantial common ground between Ted and his neighbors. Even if Christians will not agree with the conceptual analyses of the issues (as in the charge of speciesism), that should not obscure the significant common ground in simply conceding that animals are to be treated with compassion and not merely thrown to the fate of human whims. Indeed, in one step our perspective of Newkirk could shift from subversive degenerate to fellow (if somewhat misguided) fighter for animal flourishing. At the same time, she could begin to see Christians not as callous abusers of animals but rather as colaborers in a noble fight for a world of greater compassion all around.

Moral Consistency and Moral Compassion

So far we have seen that it is unfair to continue to dismiss animal rights activism as absurd, obnoxious, and dangerous. Animal rights activists are neither cognitively deficient, nor are their core values obviously morally deficient. We have already seen that there is much we need to be reminded of in terms of compassion for others. But animal rights challenges us to go beyond that initial compassionate impulse to think more carefully about our moral obligations toward animals. In this section we will initiate that process by beginning to consider how our treatment of animals is arbitrary as well as what a morally consistent and compassionate response to animals might look like.

In order to begin thinking about this problem of arbitrariness and moral consistency, let us turn our attention to the seaside Peruvian town of Huacho, nestled on the Pan American highway near beautiful

Lomas de Lachay National Park. If you visit Huacho in the summer, you just might be fortunate enough to attend its famed Guinea Pig Festival. Truly a unique event, the festival features adorably plump and chirpy little guinea pigs dressed up in a variety of elaborate miniature costumes ranging from miners to princesses. Once appropriately attired, the little creatures then compete in a one-of-a-kind fashion show. While the midday fashion show is high in the "cute factor," the end of the day is decidedly darker, as the plump losers step off the fashion runway and into the frying pan—literally. You see, the evening is capped off by a feast of rodent flesh that sees the little critters that had been dressed up in Peruvian finery only hours earlier being roasted and fried, head, feet, and all. While this event might strike the average North American guinea pig lover as cruel, even grotesque, the fact is that the guinea pig has been raised for food by the indigenous people of the Andes for hundreds of years. Nor are the Peruvians the only people to eat animals that North Americans consider pets and companions. (For instance, we can find horse on a French menu and dog on a Chinese menu.)

So why is it exactly that the consumption of guinea pigs, horses, and dogs makes North Americans uncomfortable? The question is addressed in an intriguing way in a *For Better or for Worse* cartoon strip that depicts young Michael visiting his uncle Danny's farm. As they feed the pigs, Michael asks why none of the animals on the farm have names. Uncle Danny replies matter-of-factly that naming the animals would effectively turn them into pets, and he doesn't like to eat anything he has had a personal relationship with. This direct response elicits a wide-eyed stare from Michael and perhaps a chuckle from the reader. But there is much more in Uncle Danny's observation than a mere punch line. Indeed, his explanation reflects a deep tension in the way we treat animals. At first blush the problem concerns the sheer arbitrariness of the farmer's actions. Danny and his family choose some animals to be pets and others to be lunch. Which animal is chosen to be a pet and which is chosen to be a meal seems to depend on nothing more than whim or circumstance.

The problem is hardly limited to Danny and his farm. People commonly treat one animal as a subject or a "thou" that they share a mutually bonded relationship with, while they treat another animal as an object or an "it" that can be eaten without a second thought. North Americans have decided that guinea pigs are to be among those animals considered as pets (or even members of the family) along with horses and dogs. At the same time, we consider certain domesticated animals like chickens, pigs, and cows to be livestock that we subject to lives of misery without a second thought. It is comforting to think that we have solid, nonarbitrary reasons to consider one group (e.g., dogs) as worthy of being subjects, while consigning another group (e.g., chickens) to mere objects of service and slaughter. But is there any reason to think that such a line exists?

In order to sense the problem of arbitrariness more fully from the animal rights activist's perspective, imagine a family that raises shih tzus (cute, fuzzy lap dogs). When the family chooses one of the dogs to become the new beloved family pet, then *it* effectively becomes a *she.* The family takes "Snowball" on walks every day, cooks her the best food, and provides her with the best medical care. Every evening Snowball gets a tummy rub and a handful of biscuits, and once a month she gets a visit to the groomer. By contrast, the other shih tzus on the farm continue to live out miserable lives in cramped conditions, stacked up in cages in the barn. They are never let out of their cages to stretch their legs, let alone to play. Indeed, they can barely turn around in the cramped cages where they spend their entire lives, and they never see the light of day. Their only purpose is to be fattened up with a sloppy gruel as rapidly as possible until the day the farmer enters the compound, clubs them to death, butchers the corpses, and sends the meat to market. Even as this grisly event unfolds on slaughter day, Snowball frolics on the back lawn with the children.

Like most North Americans, Ted finds this story disturbing in a couple of different ways. First, as the proud owner of Scraps, he is troubled by the fact that any dogs could be treated so callously and then slaughtered for meat. In accord with North American cultural norms, Ted has always thought of dogs as pets rather than mere objectified livestock. Second, Ted is also disturbed by the arbitrariness by which the family selects one particular dog to be loved as a cherished member of the family, even as the rest continue to be treated with the most callous indifference. That intuitively seems *wrong* to Ted: How could they select one shih tzu for a reprieve while others are consigned to a horrendous fate? There is nothing wrong with arbitrarily selecting one shrub to uproot from the yard while cultivating another with fertilizer and water. But we're not talking here about shrubs: we're talking about sentient creatures, that is, conscious animals with complex emotional lives and an ability to suffer.

Ted is right. We *are* talking about sentient creatures, and that makes a difference. But even more, we are talking about creatures we can develop significant friendships with. For a good example of the deep and profound depth of the mutual bonding that is possible between human and dog, consider the case of Greyfriars Bobby. On February 15, 1858, John Gray, an employee for the Edinburgh City Police, passed away, leaving behind his two-year-old Skye terrier, Bobby. Clearly distraught over his owner's death, Bobby followed the body out to the cemetery. Then after Gray's body was interred, the little dog refused to leave. Sunshine or rain, cold or warmth, day or night, day after day the faithful little dog sat on his owner's tomb.

Eventually the kind villagers began to bring Greyfriars Bobby food, and the little dog continued to live in the graveyard for the next fourteen years. This little dog has since become a symbol for the faithfulness of our four-legged companions around the world. In 1981 the Duke of Gloucester revealed a monument of red granite stone over Bobby's grave that was inscribed with the following words:

Greyfriars Bobby
Died 14th January 1872
Aged 16 years
Let his loyalty and devotion be a lesson to us all.

The memorial is revealing, especially for those who know that dogs often demonstrate more loyalty and kindness than many human beings. The fact is well attested in the number of therapy dogs that are used to visit hospitals, retirement homes, and homeless shelters to offer people a source of comfort and conciliation, not to mention the millions of dogs (like Scraps and Snowball) that enjoy their status as beloved family pets.

There certainly is something to be said for the intuition that it is wrong to eat animals that have the potential to be wonderful companions. The basic intuition that guides us here is summarized by the activists in China who protested outside a restaurant that served cat and dog with a placard that simply read: "Cats and dogs are friends of humans. Stop eating them, please."[8] Whether or not you agree with this plea, it is certainly not in the realm of the ridiculous. Nor does it constitute anything like a wicked assault on human dignity. It is at least plausible to argue that if an animal has the potential to be our friend, we ought not eat it.

If we agree that there is something to be said for the intuition that you don't eat your friends (or your potential friends), this intuition will quickly take us further than some of us might like. The problem is that there is nothing about the animals we choose in North America (e.g., guinea pigs, dogs, horses) that uniquely qualifies these creatures as being uniquely fit for human relationship. Chickens, pigs, and cows—three species that provide the cornerstone of the industrial meat industry in North America—are also potential friends with

---

8. Richard Spencer, "Cat Activists Storm Chinese Restaurant," *Daily Telegraph* (June 19, 2006), http://www.telegraph.co.uk/news/worldnews/asia/china/1521707/ Cat-activists-storm-Chinese-restaurant.html.

YOU'RE NOT AS **CRAZY** AS I THINK

comparable intelligence and ability to bond with human beings. If we sense that it is wrong to select a shih tzu for slaughter, given that it is capable of a mutually bonded relationship with human beings, then it would also seem to be wrong to select other species for slaughter when they have an equivalent capacity for relationship. Pigs are as intelligent as dogs; they can be house trained and leash trained and are very affectionate and playful. (But be warned, they are mischievous and can learn to open the fridge in their quest for food.[9]) Chickens are also highly intelligent creatures that can learn their place in a pecking order of more than one hundred chickens, and they too are able to bond closely with human beings. Even the bovine, if too large to curl up in front of the fireplace, can nonetheless become a loved part of the family. In their natural environment cows lives in social hierarchies and experience complex emotional lives. Moreover, a cow separated from a beloved human companion will become visibly distressed. So if Ted thinks he is somehow better than the dog-eating Chinese person because he wouldn't consider eating the scraps of Scraps, he should think again. Nor are we meat-eating North Americans fit to judge the citizens of Huacho for dressing one guinea pig in a cotton pollera and another in garlic and butter, for we are no less arbitrary in our actions.

Given the nagging force of compassion, industrial agriculture has a significant vested interest in shielding the general public from the horrific conditions of industrial food production.[10] As such, it is hardly surprising that the animal rights activists are determined to get in the face of the general public by confronting people, whether they like it or not, with some of the grosser images and footage from the industry. (In this sense there are interesting parallels between the strategies of animal rights and antiabortion activists.) And for those

---

9. For more on pigs as pets, see www.potbellypigs.com.
10. See www.goveg.com/factoryFarming.asp.

who are not alienated by this rather confrontational assault on the senses evident in the Jean Paul Gaultier protest, there is much to tug on the conscience.

For an excellent example of our double standards on animals, consider the case of Michael Vick. Vick was a star quarterback in the National Football League for the Atlanta Falcons when, on April 25, 2007, a search warrant carried out on his rural Virginia property revealed an extensive dogfighting network. Over the coming weeks news emerged of Vick's participation in a dogfighting ring that frequently engaged in the abuse, torture, and execution of fighting dogs. In November 2008 Vick received a three-year suspended sentence for his activities. While the public may have disagreed about the proper punishment owing to Vick, his callous actions were unanimously condemned as barbaric, cruel, and sadistic.

In light of the overwhelming weight of public opinion, it was surprising when, on August 22, 2007, a short op-ed appeared in the *Philadelphia Daily News* titled "We're All Michael Vick."[11] "No, we're not!" many people roared back. "We love dogs!" The provocative article was written by Gary Francione, a professor of law at Rutgers School of Law and a well-known defender of animal rights. In the article Francione argued that the outrage against Vick illumines a widespread moral schizophrenia in our treatment of animals. This schizophrenia reflects the arbitrariness with which we befriend some animals and eat others. To illustrate the point Francione compared Vick to a character he called "Simon the Sadist," who derives pleasure from roasting dogs with a blowtorch. We would agree that both Simon and Vick engaged in monstrous behavior, for it is wrong to inflict suffering on dogs because doing so somehow increases our pleasure. But then Francione asked: "How are those of us who eat animal flesh and animal products any different from Simon? He enjoys blowtorching dogs—we enjoy

---

11. See Francione, "We're All Michael Vick," http://www.philly.com/dailynews/opinion/20070822_Were_all_Michael_Vick.html.

the taste of flesh and animal products. *But we and Simon both kill sentient beings* (although we may pay others to do the dirty work) *because we derive enjoyment from it*" (emphasis added).

Francione's short essay raises the question, Do we believe that it is permissible to subject animals to great suffering and death simply because it gives us pleasure? Both Vick and Simon the Sadist subjected dogs to suffering and death because it gave them pleasure. But while we judge this to be inexcusable behavior, don't we flout this principle when we subject animals to suffering and death simply for the pleasure of eating them? As Francione put it: "Michael Vick may enjoy watching dogs fight. Someone else may find that repulsive but see nothing wrong with eating an animal who has had a life as full of pain and suffering as the lives of the fighting dogs. It's strange that we regard the latter as morally different from, and superior to, the former. How removed from the screaming crowd around the dog pit is the laughing group around the summer steak barbecue?"

Francione's short article generated a tremendous response, with many people intrigued by its simple and compelling moral axiom. If it is wrong to cause animals to suffer, it is wrong for Vick to force animals to fight for his pleasure, and it is wrong for us to eat animals for our pleasure.[12] Whether or not you find this reasoning persuasive, the lesson for us is simply that there is an appreciable case of rational and moral force to be made for animal rights. And that is much more than I suspect most evangelicals have been willing to concede.

I hope it is now apparent that animal rights activists are not necessarily absurd or obnoxious, let alone dangerous. Certainly there are extremists on the fringe like the ALF, but then as we have noted, every movement (evangelicalism included) has extremists on the fringe. And

---

12. But don't we have to eat meat for a balanced diet? On the contrary, many animal rights activists argue that a vegetarian diet is actually healthier than an omnivore diet. But even if it were not, it is still undeniable that *most* of the meat we consume (e.g., the ground beef on those nachos I ate last night) is not out of dietary necessity.

as I noted above, it is always poor form to judge a broad movement by the extremist elements.

Doesn't the Bible Say We Can Eat Animals?

It seems pretty clear that animal rights activism represents a morally defensible position that deserves to be taken seriously. We can get a sense of the overarching philosophy that drives activists like Newkirk and Francione by considering the familiar word *vegetarian*. Many people assume this word comes from the word *vegetable*, a notion that seems to consign these animal rights folk to a rather bleak culinary landscape of cucumbers and carrots. But, in point of fact, the term derives from the Latin word *vegetus*, which means "life."[13] In other words, vegetarianism and animal rights with it are not ultimately concerned with cucumbers and carrots, but rather with upholding the beauty and sacredness of all life.

Many people find something attractive in this comprehensive life-affirming philosophy. Is it at least possible that an evangelical like Ted could find his neighbors' moral position to be not only respectable but even worth considering? Could they possibly persuade him to abstain from meat? The question prompts us to address the elephant in the room: Doesn't Scripture commend, and, therefore in some sense, expect the eating of meat? Certainly many Christians like Ted view the consumption of meat not only as scripturally permitted but even as an expectation or duty. As a result, even if we have persuaded Ted to sample some tofurkey (a faux turkey made of tofu) at the farmer's market, he still finds no compunction to limit himself to coleslaw at the local KFC simply because in another life that chicken could have been his friend.

---

13. A vegetarian is a person who abstains from eating animal flesh. A vegan is a person who abstains from the consumption or use of any animal products including eggs, milk, leather, and even silk.

Let's begin here: Why think that Scripture obliges people to eat meat? Perhaps the most important biblical text in favor of the "biblical barbecue" comes when God made the following promise to Noah: "The fear and dread of you will fall on all the beasts of the earth and all the birds in the sky, on every creature that moves along the ground, and on all the fish in the sea; they are given into your hands. Everything that lives and moves will be food for you. Just as I gave you the green plants, I now give you everything" (Genesis 9:2–3).

This passage seems to suggest that humans have the right to eat everything from lettuce to lemurs. Even if the Jews were given a set of dietary restrictions, they were never asked to abstain from meat altogether. And after the coming of Christ, those restrictions were no longer operative anyway. In Peter's vision God commanded him to kill and eat animals that were once considered unclean (Acts 10:13). And quite clearly Jesus was certainly no vegetarian. After all, the centerpiece of the Last Supper was the Passover lamb. And let us not forget that after his resurrection Jesus made a point of eating fish—not tofu—on the beach.

These are all legitimate points that, to my mind at least, establish the compatibility of Christian discipleship with a meat-eating diet. But even so, we would be remiss not to note that there is another set of biblical texts that provide an alternative commentary. Let's begin by going back beyond the period of Noah to the very event of creation. Here we read that God's original intention was that his creatures would not eat meat: God intended *all* his creatures to be vegetarian (Genesis 1:29–30). Thus it is only after the fall that predation and carnivory became part of the animal kingdom.[14] What is more, it is only after the Noahic flood that these practices are extended to human

---

14. Some Christians (old-earth creationists and theistic evolutionists) believe that predation and carnivory occurred even before the fall of Adam and Eve. But even if we took this position, we could still take these protological statements (i.e., statements concerning creation in its original form) as bearing an eschatological force: that is, they reflect a goal of harmony that God will one day realize.

beings as well. Just as God's original intent for creation is peace among all creatures, so is his goal for all creation. In Isaiah God provided us a glimpse of a new world, the redemption of his creation, which will be marked by the restoration of peace to animals and persons alike, a world in which even the once predatory wolf and lion will lie down with the calf and the lamb (Isaiah 11:6–9). Woody Allen once quipped that the lion might one day lie down with the lamb, but the lamb won't get much sleep. But the incredible thing is that it will. Harmony will be restored to all creatures (Isaiah 65:25). And the stain of suffering that comes with predation and death will be forever wiped away.[15]

So how should we understand the relationship between meat eating and Christian identity? Here's one possibility: vegetarianism is not a moral obligation on the Christian, but it does provide one legitimate way to anticipate the peaceable kingdom that even now God is bringing into being. Even if we are well "within our rights" to eat meat, we might nonetheless decide not to do so (or perhaps to eat less meat) as a hopeful anticipation of that future state. It is worth keeping things in perspective. Every year about fifty-three *billion* land animals are slaughtered by human beings. (Aquatic animals would greatly increase that number.) In light of all this suffering and death, it seems to me that there is something admirable about the resolve to anticipate a better world that no longer includes all that suffering and death, by abstaining from the consumption of animal products.

---

15. As my colleague Jerry Shepherd pointed out, there is one important passage of the banquet in the new creation that describes *meat* at the table: "On this mountain the Lord Almighty will prepare a feast of rich food for all peoples, a banquet of aged wine—the best of meats and the finest of wines" (Isaiah 25:6). Is this notion of carnivory in the restored kingdom of God a problem? I don't think so. For one thing, the consumption of meat does not necessarily require the suffering and death of any particular animal. In fact, PETA has offered a one-million-dollar prize to the first scientist able to grow chicken meat in a laboratory and market it successfully. If PETA can conceive of current scientists getting meat on the table apart from the slaughter of any animals, certainly God can accomplish this feat in a new creation.

Coda

It is human nature that we tend to be concerned with our own affairs, whether as individual human beings or as a species. As a result, it is perhaps not all surprising that comparatively little attention has been paid to the plight of creation. And it is therefore striking to see that in the middle of his discussion of human salvation in the book of Romans, Paul offered a truly astounding commentary on the fallenness of creation and its hope: "The creation waits in eager expectation for the children of God to be revealed. For the creation was subjected to frustration, not by its own choice, but by the will of the one who subjected it, in hope that the creation itself will be liberated from its bondage to decay and brought into the glorious freedom of the children of God" (Romans 8:19–21).

In this text Paul observed that creation was tied into the fall of humanity. Just as we fell from God, so creation, as a result, fell as well. And just as we await our liberation from bondage, so creation does as well. What does it mean for creation to be one day liberated from that bondage but that it will finally be liberated from the cycle of death (or circle of life) that has gripped it for these many millennia? Motivated by the hope of a creation in which all suffering will at last be erased, it seems that there is indeed room under the big tent of God's people for the moral witness of the evangelical vegetarian.

10

NOT ALL
ATHEISTS
ARE FOOLS

I n a 2007 Gallup poll Americans were surveyed on their willingness to vote a representative candidate from various groups as president. Ninety-four percent responded that they would consider voting for a black candidate, 88 percent for a female candidate, 67 percent for a candidate married three times, and 55 percent for a homosexual candidate. But perhaps most striking (and certainly most dismal) is the fact that only 45 percent of the population expressed the willingness to vote for an atheist.[1] With this sobering statistic, the poll demonstrated that atheists remain among the most mistrusted, feared, and discriminated-against groups in society.

As a typical evangelical, Ted would certainly be among the majority that wouldn't vote for an atheist. After all, as I noted in the introduction, he wouldn't consider hiring one to work in his sporting goods shop. Even though Osman's experience, aptitude, and references suggested that he would make a model employee, his atheism

---

1. The poll was conducted between February 9 and 11, 2007. See Jeffrey M. Jones, "Some Americans Reluctant to Vote for Mormon, 72-Year-Old Presidential Candidates,"
http://www.gallup.com/poll/26611/some-americans-reluctant-vote-mormon-72yearold-presidential-candidates.aspx.

was reason enough for Ted to throw out his application. And if you were to ask Ted why he dismissed Osman's application, his response would be unequivocal and unapologetic: any person who denies that there is a God is either irredeemably stupid or (more likely) in sinful rebellion against God. Either way, Ted is certainly not going to hire such a person to sell bicycles and baseball gloves.

But how can Ted make such a sweeping claim that *all* atheists are either stupid or wicked? How does he know that this explains Osman's disbelief in particular? Ted will readily admit that he does not know any atheists personally, so his information cannot come from firsthand experience. Instead, it derives from his reading of Scripture. Ted reads in Psalm 19:1–2 that "the heavens declare the glory of God; the skies proclaim the work of his hands. Day after day they pour fourth speech; night after night they display knowledge." Ted believes that this passage is straightforward and unequivocal: the beauty, order, and complexity of creation are amply on display, testifying to the handiwork of God as the Creator. Thus the person who denies this testimony either is malfunctioning at a basic level or is refusing to acknowledge that which he clearly perceives.

The bumper sticker on Ted's Audi smugly declares: "April 1st is Atheist Day." The allusion is to Psalm 14:1, which declares with admirable directness: "Fools say in their hearts, 'There is no God.'" While some atheists may take this view because of cognitive malfunction, Ted believes that we find in the apostle Paul a darker explanation of disbelief rooted in human rebellion: "For since the creation of the world God's invisible qualities—his eternal power and divine nature—have been clearly seen, being understood from what has been made, so that people are without excuse. For although they knew God, they neither glorified him as God nor gave thanks to him, but their thinking became futile and their foolish hearts were darkened" (Romans 1:20–21).

Paul seems to have been claiming that some people hear and see the testimony of God and yet *refuse to acknowledge* what their senses clearly reveal. Consider the following scenario. Imagine that you're walking in the woods with a friend one dark night when you suddenly hear a roar in the darkness. "Did you hear that?" you cry to your friend, but he shakes his head and looks at you strangely. Moments later you see a light flash just over the crest of the hill so bright that it illumines the surrounding forest with the brilliance of the noonday sun. "Did you see that?" you whisper in awe to your friend. But he throws another strange look your way and shakes his head. A second later the ground beneath you shudders from a massive impact. "Did you feel that?" you shout out to your friend, but he just stares blankly back at you as if you're crazy. What would you think of your friend's reaction (or lack thereof) to this succession of stupendous sensory stimuli? Either he is for some reason unable to sense these phenomena or else he did sense them but for some reason—mischievousness? stubbornness?—he refuses to acknowledge them. Ted finds himself left with similarly blunt options. Is Osman fundamentally unable to process certain perceptual facts about the world, or does he perceive them and yet refuse to acknowledge them? Either way, we can understand Ted's reluctance to hire this atheist. By the same token, we can understand the reluctance of a majority of the American population to elect an atheist to the highest office in the land. After all, would you consider voting for a presidential candidate you believed to be either stupid or wicked?

In this chapter we are going to lend the same charitable ear to atheists that we have offered to our other groups. And in keeping with previous chapters, I shall focus the discussion on challenging the central assumption that an atheist must be stupid and/or wicked. I shall do so in two steps. In the first step we will consider how people often adopt an atheist position at least in part because of the distorted witness of Christians. As a result, at least some atheists might actually be directing their unbelief at one or another distortion of the faith. In the second section we shall consider the most significant reason that atheists adopt their position: the problem of evil. I believe that when we understand the complexity introduced by these two factors—the distorted conceptions of God possessed by many atheists and the shattering impact of the problem of evil—we will come to appreciate how important it is to seek to understand a person like Osman rather than assuming that he must be either stupid or wicked.

Which God Don't You Believe In?

Before launching into a full-on apologetical assault on the atheist, the thoughtful Christian will pause to ask this clichéd but nonetheless essential question: "Tell me about the God you don't believe in, because I probably don't believe in that God either." As simplistic, and even trite, as this comment might first appear, it contains an important insight. Before you begin to attack the atheist's disbelief, you ought to find out which God he disbelieves in because you may not believe in that God either. As we will see, people can have a distorted view owing as much to false practices as to false doctrines.

Let's begin with a particular historical example for which we must travel back to the sixteenth century. This brings us to Bartolomé de Las Casas's firsthand account of the Spanish occupation of Latin America. Las Casas records numerous details of the horrific genocide and innumerable specific atrocities wrought by the conquistadors:

> They attacked the towns and spared neither the children nor the aged nor pregnant women nor women in childbed, not only stabbing them and dismembering them but cutting them to pieces as if dealing with sheep in the slaughter house. They laid bets as to who, with one stroke of the sword, could split a man in two or could cut off his head or spill out his entrails with a single stroke of the pike. They took infants from their mothers' breasts, snatching them by the legs and pitching them headfirst against the crags or snatched them by the arms and threw them into the rivers, roaring with laughter and saying as

the babies fell into the water, "Boil there, you offspring of the devil!"[2]

This horrific genocide, carried out under the banner of pious Spanish Catholicism, was the first contact thousands of indigenous peoples had with Christianity. And as such it provides the sobering backdrop for our present case.

With that sobering prologue we now turn to the encounter between a native cacique (that is, a tribal leader) named Hatuey and his Franciscan Catholic captors. In this encounter Hatuey has been told he will be executed, apparently for no greater crime than not being Spanish. But all is not lost, for the Franciscans benevolently provided Hatuey with the opportunity to save his soul prior to the destruction of his body: "When tied to the stake, the cacique Hatuey was told by a Franciscan friar who was present, an artless rascal, something about the God of the Christians and of the articles of Faith. And he was told what he could do in the brief time that remained to him, in order to be saved and go to heaven."[3] And how did Hatuey respond? "The cacique, who had never heard any of this before, and was told he would go to Inferno where, if he did not adopt the Christian Faith, he would suffer eternal torment, asked the Franciscan friar if Christians all went to Heaven. When told that they did *he said he would prefer to go to Hell*."[4]

This story powerfully illustrates the importance of clarifying what a person is rejecting when he or she rejects God or the gospel. On the face of it you would reasonably assume that a person who replied to a gospel presentation with the wish that he would prefer to go to hell

---

2. Las Casas, "The Devastation of the Indies: A Brief Account," *Voices of a People's History of the United States*, eds. Anthony Arnove and Howard Zinn (New York: Seven Stories Press, 2004), 38–9.

3. Las Casas, "The Devastation of the Indies: A Brief Account," 41.

4. Las Casas, "The Devastation of the Indies: A Brief Account," 41, emphasis added.

was a hopeless rebel. After all, what kind of person would ever choose hell over heaven? And yet once we hear of Hatuey's circumstances and just how distorted his understanding of Christianity was, it should be obvious that he was not really wishing for hell. Indeed, based on the fact that the Spanish Christians were acting more like demons, it seems likely that Hatuey's wish for hell constituted not an obstinate rejection of a merciful offer of salvation but rather a morally praise-worthy rejection of the evils the conquistadors were perpetuating in the name of God.

Theologian George Lindbeck captured this point in a famous il-lustration in which he described a Christian crusader yelling, "*Christus est dominus!*" (Christ is Lord!) just prior to cleaving the skull of a hap-less Muslim with his mace.[5] Lindbeck claimed that in this context the crusader's proclamation was false. But how could that be correct? Isn't "Jesus is Lord" always true? The answer is simple: it is not true if what a person *means* when he or she says "Jesus is Lord" has changed. And the context of our statements often tips us off that the mean-ing has changed. The crusader's genocidal actions that accompany his words suggest that he meant something like this: "My God, who commands me to slay all infidels without mercy, is Lord!" And this means that when a crusader cries out Christ's lordship just prior to killing a Muslim, he is *not saying the same thing* as a bishop who says, "Christ is Lord," in church or a man who says it as he feeds the poor. By the same token, the man who says, "The police are corrupt," while on vacation in Tijuana may say something true, while the man who says, "The police are corrupt," when back home in Vancouver says something false.

Now is it any surprise that the Muslim child who witnessed his father getting his head bashed in by this bloodthirsty crusading lout will want nothing to do with this Jesus? We can readily picture the

---

5. Lindbeck, *The Nature of Doctrine: Religion and Theology in a Postliberal Age* (Philadelphia: Westminster Press, 1984), 64.

Muslim child standing over the corpse of his father, tears streaming down his cheeks as he resolutely declares that *Jesus is* not *Lord*. Surely the context of this event and the portrayal of Jesus that he is reacting against should be considered before we consider the boy a hopeless rebel. If the boy thinks of Jesus as the cruel, violent warlord who ordered the killing of his daddy, then "Jesus is Lord" is indeed false. And if Hatuey thinks of heaven as a retirement home for hateful, genocidal maniacs, then is it surprising that he would sooner go to hell?

Such cases leave us to wonder how many people might reject God in name when in fact they are actually rejecting only a deeply distorted presentation of God that they have received from the words and deeds of others. Could it be that the atheist might sometimes even function as an unwitting prophet by rejecting a particularly unfaithful witness to God and the gospel? Inquiring into the reasons that people adopt an atheist position can be deeply disconcerting, not least when we discover how much of that disbelief traces back to failures arising in the church. Alas, examples are not hard to come by. The early church historian Elaine Pagels attended a very conservative church when she was in high school, but all that changed when she lost a beloved friend:

> [T]he leaders of the church I attended directed their charges not to associate with outsiders, except to convert them. Then, after a close friend was killed in an automobile accident at the age of sixteen, my fellow evangelicals commiserated but declared that, since he was Jewish and not "born again," he was eternally damned. Distressed and disagreeing with their interpretation—and finding no room for discussion—I realized that I was no longer at home in their world and left that church.[6]

---

6. Elaine Pagels, *Beyond Belief: The Secret Gospel of Thomas* (New York: Random House, 2003), 31.

It may be that Pagels was alienated as much by the uncompromising and unpastoral way the church expressed its views—your friend's in hell, case closed—as by its actual assessment. (This is a good reminder that the source of alienation often lies as much with how we say something as with what it is we say.) While Pagels never took that final step to atheism, many people have become atheists after similar cases of hurt, disappointment, and pastoral insensitivity. Such cases must always remind us to ask which God it is that people who leave the church are rejecting.

There would appear to be many cases where people become atheists because of the unloving actions of those in the church. But people also reject the church because of deeply flawed understandings of Christian doctrine. As I reflect on my own upbringing, I can identify numerous teachings and experiences that, to say the least, were very damaging to a proper understanding of God. For instance, I grew up reading Jack Chick tracts. Although I know little about Jack Chick himself (though still producing tracts in his eighties, he is a famously reclusive personality), from a young age I became familiar with his little cartoon booklets that conveyed what I now recognize to be a hyperfundamentalist Christian faith. I would find them on the "tract racks" of a family restaurant where we would sometimes go for breakfast. I could also get them at the local Christian bookstore where they cost a quarter. And they would occasionally turn up among the stacks of the *Four Spiritual Laws* at church. (Always a treasured find!) As a kid I liked collecting Chick tracts for their macabre themes replete with angels and demons as well as their engaging cartoon format. But looking back now, I see that while these tracts reflect some gospel truths, they also often represent a vicious and insular concept of Christian faith. Few individuals escape the attack of Jack Chick as his booklets lampoon evolutionists, atheists, homosexuals, Catholics, and just about anybody else who does not buy into his narrow brand of fundamentalism. Although many people have undoubtedly been saved through Jack Chick's hard work, it has not come without a cost.

One of Jack Chick's most disturbing tracts is called *Somebody Goofed*. In this tract an older man befriends an impressionable young man at a party. As they are driving along after the party, the older man goads his young friend on, challenging him to speed up in order to beat the oncoming train. Clearly impressionable and eager to please, the young man foolishly takes his friend's advice. While he thinks he can beat the train, tragically he is *dead wrong* (sorry, I couldn't resist) as it slams into the car, killing both men. In the next panel we see both men in the flames of hell, at which point the older man smugly informs the younger man that since he failed to accept Jesus as his Savior he is now consigned to hell for eternity. With the realization of what he missed slowly dawning, the young man pleads for another chance to accept Jesus as his Savior, but the older man smugly replies that it is now too late. Upon hearing this news, the young man points a quivering finger at the older man and screams, "You goofed!" "*No*," the older man replies as he begins to pull off a face mask, revealing a terrifying demonic visage underneath, "*you goofed. You didn't accept Jesus Christ as your Savior!*" Game over. With that the demon begins to laugh and taunt the young man who foolishly attempted to outrun a 250-ton diesel train and has ended up eternally damned as a result.[7]

As a child reading Jack Chick, I thought that this was a reasonably accurate presentation of the gospel. Thus if you missed your opportunity for repentance—even if it was out of the trickery of an undercover demon—that was it. One serious goof would be enough to damn you for eternity. Eventually I outgrew this cruel and distorted view of Christianity. I now look back on Chick's teachings as representing (for all his sincerity) a repugnant and medieval distortion of the doctrine of hell and a perversion of the love and justice of God. But how many people have this distorted conception of Christianity—from a

---

7. "Somebody Goofed" is available at http://www.chick.com/reading/tracts/0003/0003_01.asp.

Chick tract or a fundamentalist pastor or an angry neighbor—and never manage to leave it behind? How many find negative experiences cementing a conception of Christianity that ultimately leads them to reject the church? What about those young people who experience the pain of Elaine Pagels upon losing a friend and being told that he or she is burning for eternity because "somebody goofed"? What about those who are kept away from the faith by some bad theology and behavior of Christians until one day they wake up atheists?

Let's pursue further this idea of people becoming atheists because of flawed (or corrupt) Christians and a flawed (or corrupt) presentation of Christianity. Consider the fictional (but possibly true) case of Hans, a Christian who was born in Germany in 1925. Hans grew up in an insular, intolerant Lutheran church through which he came to associate "God" with dead orthodoxy, legalism, and anti-Semitism. His minister often preached that the misfortunes of Germany were God's judgment for showing toleration of the Christ-killing Jews. Then came that horrid pogrom known as Kristallnacht on November 9, 1938. On that chaotic night Hans saw the neighborhood synagogue burned to the ground and a number of Jews, including some beloved childhood friends, beaten in the streets and deported to concentration camps. On the following Sunday Hans's pastor praised the mobs in a blazing sermon where he proclaimed God's impending judgment against the cursed brood of Jews. Disgusted by this reprehensible display of anti-Semitism, Hans finally left the Lutheran church. Unaware of the beleaguered confessing church, which, in its strident rejection of anti-Semitism, offered a respite for Christians of conscience, he came to believe that Christianity was inextricably linked to the Third Reich. Though he wanted to believe in the existence of God, the only God Hans had known was one who approves the persecution of Jewish grandmothers and toddlers. Finally, in 1944 Hans joined a group of anti-Nazi insurgents, all of whom were atheists. By this point, weary of religion and talk of God, Hans found their atheism as natural and morally admirable as their anti-Nazism.

Hans was no fool, certainly not in the way that many Christians like Ted think of atheists. He was a very intelligent and thoughtful individual, independently minded, and certainly the intellectual and moral superior of the average pro-Nazi German Lutheran. You cannot attribute his atheism to a cognitive deficit. Nor does it seem plausible to explain his atheism as an expression of moral rebellion against God. On the contrary, he was standing against the horrors of German state Christianity in a way starkly reminiscent of Hatuey's stance against the conquistadors. So when Hans told his shocked pastor that he'd prefer to go to (Jewish) hell than (German) heaven, he was not wishing damnation but rather raising an indictment against German Christianity, as surely as Hatuey raised an indictment against Spanish Christianity.

Both Hatuey and Hans force us to rethink quick judgments against the "recalcitrant rebel." Indeed, both cases force us to ask whether some people who adopt an avowedly atheistic position could possibly be morally *praiseworthy* for doing so. After all, if a person's understanding of Christianity is as radically distorted as that conveyed to Hatuey and Hans, wouldn't they seem admirable as they reveal a courageous willingness to stand apart from the hordes, often at significant personal risk, to confess disbelief in this tyrannical deity? In this case the tragedy lies not with their "disbelief" but rather with the fundamentally corrupt conception of God that they rejected. And so our focus of judgment shifts from the atheists to the Christians who make them.

Does God Make Atheists?

In chapter three we discussed the problem of evil as an example of the Christian confirmation bias. I agreed that Christians often fail to appreciate the depth of the intellectual and pastoral problems that evil poses to Christian belief. In light of what was argued in the last section, is it possible that people could have experiences with evil that they find irreconcilable with their conception of God such that choosing atheism is intellectually and even morally reasonable? Thinking of Osman specifically, my concern is not to establish that his atheism is intellectually or morally justified, but rather that, for all we know, it *could* be. With that point of inquiry in mind, let's begin to think about Osman in the same way that we have thought about the "impious" beliefs of Hatuey and Hans.

Let's begin by situating Osman's disbelief. For all its moral progress in certain areas, the twentieth century is also the great century of genocides, including the Armenians, Jews, Cambodians, Kurds, Tutsis, and many others. And each of these horrible events is itself an aggregate of countless particular acts of unspeakable brutality and evil. In some cases the evil is so extreme and cruel as literally to defy our imaginations. Consider Bosnia 1994, one of the lesser-known genocides but certainly one of the most vicious. In researching this genocide I read one haunting account that described a grandfather who was forced to witness the murder and disembowelment of his grandson. And if that were not horrific enough, the perpetrators then *forced the grandfather to eat some of his grandson's intestines* before they finally killed the poor wretch by impaling him to a tree.

Now a simple question: How is a person to maintain faith in a perfectly loving and all-powerful God in light of evils such as this? As we saw in chapter three, the primary theodicy to explain why God allows evil comes down to an appeal to greater goods. In short, it is argued that God foreordained that this grandchild would be disemboweled and that his grandfather would be forced to eat his entrails and then impaled to a tree because allowing these events would lead to a sum total greater good on balance than would have occurred if the child and his grandfather had enjoyed serene and trouble-free lives. Even if no Christian theodicist would dare speculate on what specific goods could possibly be achieved through such a horrifying event as this, we are told that there must be some compensating goods. We could simply choose to accept on faith that this is the case. But what if, upon reflecting on the horror of the case, a person becomes convinced that there just *could not* be adequately compensating goods for an evil this heinous? I can certainly understand how somebody could come to this conclusion. And if they did, then they would have a reason that they could no longer be a theist. The existence of this single unjustifiable evil could be sufficient for them to conclude that there is no God.

With that possibility in mind, let's turn our attention to Osman. What if the horrifying Bosnian murder was part of Osman's family history? What if the two victims were Osman's brother and grandfather? Then consider that after these horrifying events Osman left for America as a deeply traumatized teenager. Though raised in the Eastern Orthodox Christian faith, he found that he could not reconcile this once deeply held faith with the horrors he experienced. In this case, Osman's experience is similar to that of Hans. After a long struggle with the trauma of losing his beloved brother and grandfather under these unthinkable conditions, he concludes that God does not exist. In other words, Osman simply cannot consider that a loving God could possibly allow the horrible fate of his brother and grandfather. Could somebody really judge his disbelief as necessarily evidence of stupidity or rebellion? Shouldn't it instead reduce us to tears?

Sadly, the world is filled with many other horrors that precipitate crises of faith in people. In the documentary *Deliver Us from Evil*, we meet two parents, once faithful Catholics, who discovered that their grown child (now a thirty-nine-year-old woman) was, for several years, raped by the family's trusted Catholic priest. To add horrifying insult to unspeakable injury, many times the parents had invited the priest to sleep over, never imagining in their worst nightmares that every night he was raping their daughter just down the hall from their room. Clearly the guilt, regret, and anguish that they experience are beyond what most of us can fathom. And in the light of that hellish realization, they respond very differently. While the mother appears to have retained her Catholic faith, the father states for the camera, with considerable anger and conviction, that there is no God.[8] While we might admire the mother's faith, does that mean that the father's conclusion is necessarily irrational or immoral? Perhaps instead of judging him, we would do better to look in the mirror and ask whether our faith could survive such a discovery.

Let's keep in mind the point above about "Jesus is Lord" changing meaning in different contexts. Could it be that there is something similar for "there is no God"? Obviously there is a trivial sense where this is true. If my only understanding of God is of an old man in the sky who hurls thunderbolts at you when you mess up, then when I declare, "There is no God," what I say is true because there is no such being as that. But I'm thinking of a subtler point than that. Is it possible that an atheist could have a much more sophisticated (and correct) concept of God and still warrant our sympathy with reference to her atheism? Take Osman for instance. He and I might agree that if there is a God, that God is all-loving and all-powerful. In that sense his view is much clearer than the man who says God is an old man in the sky. Where the problem arises is that Osman thinks of that horrible day that his brother and grandfather were killed and concludes that no God who is all-loving and all-powerful would stand aside while such a horror unfolded. Bob Jyono, the father in *Deliver Us from Evil*, seemed to reason in like manner when he contemplated the possibility that God might have stood by passively for several years while his daughter was raped. No, that just cannot be. No God would allow *that*.

We can put it like this. The Christian, Osman, and Mr. Jyono all agree that if God exists, God is all-powerful and all-loving, and, defined that way, God would never allow an evil to occur unless it would bring about a greater good. Where the difference lies is that Osman and Mr. Jyono do not believe that God *could* achieve a justifying greater good

---

8. I discuss this case in *Finding God in the Shack* (Colorado Springs, CO: Paternoster, 2009), 115–116.

for the horrific evils they have witnessed. If this analysis is possibly true—and it certainly seems to me that it is not only possibly true but that in many cases it is quite plausible—then it would follow that people like Osman and Mr. Jyono are atheists not out of an ignorant or rebellious will but rather out of the belief that there could be no compensating justifying good for the evils they have witnessed and/or experienced. In light of this understanding, to say, "There is no God," is to say, "There is no God who would allow unjustified evils." And on that point at least, the Christian and atheist would find themselves in agreement.

We could push this analysis a bit further yet with the possibility that in some cases an atheist's disbelief could actually arise from pious considerations. Let's begin with the following analogy. Imagine that your neighbor Mr. Grady is a breeder of cute, fuzzy shih tzus. You have seen Grady work with the dogs for years, and you have always known him to be a kind, gentle, and caring soul. Many times you have recommended Grady to people seeking to purchase a puppy. Then one day you return home and see Grady's house cordoned off with police tape and several police cars in the driveway. One of the officers outside the house tells you that all the dogs were discovered with their throats slit and their bodies mutilated. Further, Grady's wall safe has been emptied, his car is gone, and a note has been discovered, apparently signed by Grady himself, stating that while he loved his dogs, he became convinced that a greater good required him to allow somebody to kill them.

Not everybody was especially fond of Grady. Indeed, Grady's son, who cared nothing for the man but eagerly anticipated inheriting a piece of his estate, is anxious to have him declared dead. So the son pleads with the officers and the district attorney that the evidence suggests that Grady was killed by invaders who staged the scene to pin the blame on the old man. While Grady's son is anxious to have him declared dead out of hostility, ambivalence, and greed, you too believe that he should be declared dead, but for a very different reason. From your perspective, it is simply *inconceivable* that Grady could have carried out these violent actions against his own beloved dogs. Nor are you convinced that he would have been complicit in anybody else acting out so violently against his dogs. You are convinced that Grady would not have any greater good here, and thus he would not let this happen. As a result, painful though it may be, you conclude that the only way to explain the horror of the scene is by concluding that Grady was killed: *he must be dead because if living he would never have permitted this to happen.*

There may well be many atheists like Grady's son who are atheists at least in part because they are ambivalent or even hostile toward God. Along these lines atheistic philosopher Thomas Nagel candidly wrote: "It isn't just that I don't believe in God and, naturally, hope that I'm right in my belief. It's that I hope there is no God! I don't want there to be a God; I don't want the universe to be like that."[9] But even conceding the motivations of these folk, mightn't there be other atheists who find their atheism a bitter pill to swallow and are forced there not by any hostility toward God per se but rather by their inability to accept the idea that God would allow the types of evil and suffering that we see in the world? If Osman and Mr. Jyono reason in this way, we may not agree, but can we not at least sympathize with their decision?

Let's imagine that in the interview Ted had pressed Osman on the reasons for his atheism. How might that conversation have gone? Let's join their conversation for a few minutes:

---

9. Nagel, *The Last Word* (Oxford: Oxford University Press, 1997), 130. Nagel does not give an in-depth analysis of his preference for atheism. However, it would be possible that someone like Osman could make these statements while thinking that a God who planned the horrors he experienced could not be a good God. Thus, he might be reasoning that no God at all is better than a capricious God. As a result, even Nagel's words cannot necessarily be taken to be expressions of unremitting hostility and rebellion against the Christian conception of God.

Ted: "Have you read Lee Strobel's *The Case for a Creator?* It's a great book that lays out all the evidence for God. My friend read it, and even though he was a doubter, he agreed afterward that God exists, as plainly as the nose on his face."

Osman: "No, I haven't read that book, but I just don't believe there could be a god."

T: "But why, if you don't mind my asking?"

O: "Well, my brother and grandfather were brutally murdered in 1994 in Bosnia. And the killers tortured my grandfather before he died as well. I really would prefer not to say any more of the horrid details. But I'll say this. After I saw them endure those horrors, I concluded that a perfectly loving and powerful God would never allow such a horrifying evil as this to occur."

T: "I am terribly sorry to hear that. I cannot imagine what it would be like to lose loved ones like that, and under such horrific circumstances."

O: "It haunts me to this day."

T: "But I don't think that this means God doesn't exist. I think he was with your brother and grandfather when they died. And, difficult though this may be, I think he must have had a reason to allow something so horrible. We may not understand the reason this side of eternity, but someday we will be able to look back from heaven and see why God allowed such a terrible event to occur."

I believe that Ted is right; I certainly hope and pray that he is. But is this point of disagreement over Osman's struggles of faith sufficient to eliminate Osman as a candidate for the sales position? Does it really suggest that Osman would not be a good employee? I don't see that this follows at all. Osman believes he can see that God could not have a justifying reason to allow this evil. What if, rather than offering quick solutions or avoiding those who are suffering, we came and sat in the ashes with them for a while, mourning the pain in the world? How might that transform the dialogue between atheists like Osman and Christians like Ted?

With that we shift from those who have themselves faced great evil to a general observation. Could we as Christians concede that there is some ambiguity in our experience of the world? That is, could we concede that while some facts support the providential hand of God being active in the universe, maybe others do not? Journalist and popular new atheist Christopher Hitchens wrote as follows:

> After the terrible Asian tsunami of 2005, and after the inundation of New Orleans in 2006, quite serious and learned men such as the archbishop of Canterbury were reduced to the level of stupefied peasants when they publicly agonized over how to interpret god's will in the matter. But if one makes the simple assumption, based on absolutely certain knowledge, that we live on a planet that is still cooling, has a molten core, faults and cracks in its crust, and a turbulent weather system, then there is simply no need for any such anxiety. Everything is already explained. I fail to see why the religious are so reluctant to admit this: it would free them from all the futile questions about why god permits so much suffering. But apparently this annoyance is a small price to pay in order to keep alive the myth of divine intervention.[10]

Why did the tsunami sweep close to a quarter million people to a watery grave? Why was a grandfather forced to cannibalize his grandson? What if a Christian would restrain himself or herself from offering apologetic responses to these pained queries and instead spend some time sitting in the ashes of the world's destruction while sharing the tears of the world's grief? What if we dared to become incarnate in the world's pain just as Christ became incarnate for us? I

---

10. Hitchens, *God Is Not Great: How Religion Poisons Everything* (New York: Twelve, 2007), 148–9.

suspect we might find a stronger argument for Christian faith than all the apologists could hope to muster.

Coda

When Ted considers an atheist like Osman, he sees a threat, a challenge, and (though he probably wouldn't admit this) a potential trophy. (After all, converting an atheist is even more prestigous than converting a Democrat.) He is not as likely to see a person with a story that might explain the genesis of doubt and that might even provide appreciable intellectual and moral grounds for that doubt. We certainly do not need to defend God. Why God allows the Bosnian horror and countless other equally terrible events, we shall never know in this life. But one thing the church can do is use atheism as a starting point for reflection. To what extent does the church provide a sober explanation for the disbelief of Hans or Hatuey? Atheists have often made the point that Christians have failed in their role as faithful witnesses to the gospel. Bertrand Russell observed that "the teaching of Christ, as it appears in the Gospels, has had extraordinarily little to do with the ethics of Christians."[11] True enough. And as I have argued, the first radical step in understanding the other comes in listening. What if Ted had withheld judgment on Osman, opting instead to learn about him and his story? Would he still be so quick to dismiss him as a fool?

---

11. Russell, "Has Religion Made Useful Contributions to Civilization?" in *Why I Am Not a Christian and Other Essays on Religion and Related Subjects,* ed. Paul Edwards (New York: Simon and Schuster, 1957), 25.

CONCLUSION ◀

TRUTH
IS ENOUGH

We began this book with the sadly misdirected piety of Sol, who obstinately resolved to choose God over truth. No Christian who seeks to model his or her life on Christ could possibly agree with that statement. If we want to be like Christ, then we must resolve always to pursue the truth, no matter what the cost to our present beliefs. That brings us back to the case of Jonathan Weber, which we encountered in chapter seven. To recap, Weber is a Harvard-trained professor in the novel *A Skeleton in God's Closet* who sees his faith come under threat with the discovery of Christ's remains in the tomb of Joseph of Arimathea. After a significant struggle over the evidence, Weber concludes:

> While gazing across the Old City, Harvard's motto came, suddenly, incongruously, to mind: *VERITAS,* truth. *Let the Yalies cling to their LUX ET VERITAS,* Jon mused, *their "Light and Truth." Truth is enough. Light, without truth, is no light at all.* Nothing—however ancient, grand, magnificent, or sustaining—must ever, *ever* stand in the way of Truth. Truth in the past, in the present, in the future.[1]

---

1. Paul Maier, *A Skeleton in God's Closet* (Nashville: Westbow, 1994), 256.

Weber is right. *Truth is enough.* And that means that we must always choose truth, whatever, whenever, however, and in whomever it manifests itself. That includes witnessing to the truth of our beliefs and listening to the truth to be found in others. As for those others, they may be liberal Christians, Darwinists, animal rights activists, or atheists. Or they could be materialists, Buddhists, communists, or anarchists. Regardless of the person, we need to view every case and every conversation as an opportunity to meet others and encounter the truth in that situation. Admittedly, this is often not easy, particularly if we have grown accustomed to retrenching in our opinions and marginalizing the other. So let's begin small. You don't have to get into lofty discussions of metaphysics and theology just yet. Instead, just lay down your weapon for a time and climb out of the trench. Then walk out onto the field of battle, not with a secret arsenal of argumentative weapons but with an invitation for coffee and a willingness to talk and listen. You just might be surprised where the conversation takes you.

ALSO AVAILABLE

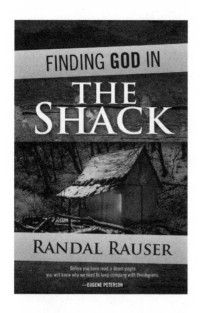

WHAT WOULD IT BE LIKE to lose your youngest child to a serial killer? And then to have God invite you out for a conversation at the very shack where the terrible deed took place? And then imagine that the door to that shack of horrors opened . . . and before you knew it you had been swept up in the motherly embrace of a large African-American woman? This most unlikely of stories, as told in William Young's *The Shack*, has become a runaway bestseller, and it is easy to see why. But even as lives have been transformed through this book, other readers have sternly denounced it as a hodgepodge of serious theological error, even heresy. With one pastor urging his congregation to read it and another forbidding his congregation to, many Christians have simply been left confused.

Aware of both the excitement and the uncertainty generated by *The Shack*, theologian Randal Rauser takes the reader on a fascinating journey through the pages of the story. In successive chapters he explores many of the book's complex and controversial issues, from why God the Father is revealed as an African-American woman, to questions of the Trinity, to the ever-vexing problem of evil. Through these chapters Rauser offers an honest and illuminating discussion that opens up a new depth to the conversation while providing the reader with new opportunities for *Finding God in The Shack*.

Paperback, 161 pages, 5.5 x 8.5
ISBN: 978-1-60657-032-6
Retail: $14.99

Available for purchase online or through your local bookstore.

ALSO AVAILABLE

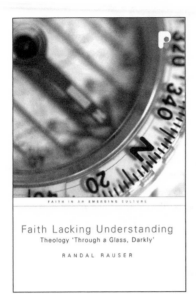

FAITH IN AN EMERGING CULTURE

Faith Lacking Understanding
Theology 'Through a Glass, Darkly'

RANDAL RAUSER

In an attempt to put mystery back at the heart of Christian theology, Rauser leads the reader on a riveting and, at times, unsettling journey through the major doctrines encapsulated in the Apostles' Creed.

In each case he illustrates how a theoretical understanding of the doctrine as yet eludes us. We simply do not know, for example, what it means for God to be Trinity, or how Christ can be both human and divine, or how the atonement works.

Rauser shows that the journey of thinking theologically which arises out of a love for and worship of God within a communal atmosphere is as important as the end result of achieving doctrines that approximate reality.

In this way the author seeks to steer us on a middle course between the twin errors of evangelicalism (heightening the doctrine) and liberalism (heightening the process).

Paperback, 206 pages, 5.5 x 8.5
ISBN: 978-1-84227-547-4
Retail: $17.99

Available for purchase online or through your local bookstore.